The
Story of Jesus:

Past, Present and Future

J. Carl Laney

Dedication

To my seminary professors who taught me the delight of personal study of God's Word.

"More desirable than gold, yes, than much fine gold; sweeter also than honey and the drippings of the honeycomb." (Psalm 19:10)

"A disciple is not above his teacher; but everyone, after he has been fully trained, will be like his teacher." Jesus (Luke 6:40)

Copies of this book available from Kindle Publishers, Amazon.com and Amazon.co.uk.

Table of Contents

Preface   9

Part 1 *What Jesus Does*

1. The Life of Christ Before Birth   12

   Jesus Creating the Universe   15
   Jesus Visiting with Abraham   17
   Jesus Wrestling with Jacob   18
   Jesus Leading Israel through the Wilderness   19
   Jesus Revealing Himself to Moses   21
   Jesus Commanding Joshua   22
   Jesus Encouraging Gideon   23
   Jesus Announcing Samson's Birth   24
   Jesus Calling Isaiah to Ministry   25
   Jesus Comforting Daniel's Friends   26
   Jesus Shutting the Lions' Mouths   28
   Jesus Cleansing Israel's High Priest   31

2. The Life of Christ On Earth   35

   Jesus' Virgin Birth   35
   Jesus' Early Years in Nazareth   37
   Jesus' Approval at His baptism   40
   Jesus' Testing through Temptation   41
   Jesus' Offer of the Kingdom   43

Jesus' Authentication by Miracles   45
Jesus' Feeding the Five Thousand   47
Jesus' Cleansing the Temple   50
Jesus' Encounter with Nicodemus   51
Jesus' Conversation with the Samaritan   54
Jesus' Appointment of the Twelve   57
Jesus' Sermon on the Mount   59
Jesus' Kingdom Ethics   61
Jesus' Teaching on Prayer   64
Jesus' Rejection by Israel   66
Jesus' Teaching the Kingdom Parables   69
Jesus' Promise to Build the Church   70
Jesus' Transfiguration   72
Jesus' Royal Entry into Jerusalem   74
Jesus' Predictions about Israel's Future   75
Jesus' Last Passover   78
Jesus' Arrest and Trial   81
Jesus' Crucifixion   84
Jesus' Death for Sin   88
Jesus' Burial in a Borrowed Tomb   89
Jesus' Resurrection before Witnesses   91
Jesus' Commissioning His Disciples   92
Jesus' Return to Heaven   95

3. The Life of Christ in Heaven   97

Jesus, Enjoying Fellowship with His Father   98
Jesus, Preparing a Place for His Followers   99
Jesus, Officiating in Heaven's Sanctuary   100

Jesus, Interceding for Believers 102
Jesus, Answering the Prayers of His People 104
Jesus, Defending Believers from Our Accuser 105
Jesus, Ruling and Gifting His Church 107
Jesus, Receiving Worship in the Heavenly Court 109

4. The Life of Christ in Prophecy 113

Jesus Will Meet Believers at the Rapture 114
Jesus Will Initiate the Tribulation Judgments 116
Jesus Will Return to Claim His Throne 118
Jesus Will Rule His Promised Kingdom 122
Jesus Will Judge Satan and His Followers 124
Jesus Will Officiate at the Final Judgment 125
Jesus Will Comfort and Bless His People 128
Jesus Will Reverse the Curse of Sin. 131
Jesus Will Welcome Worship and Service 134

Part 2 *What Jesus Says*

About Accountability 137
About Anxiety 139
About the Church 140
About Compassion 141
About Discipleship 142
About Demons 144
About His Deity 145
About Divorce 146
About Faith 148

About Fasting — 148
About Family — 150
About Fear — 151
About Forgiveness — 152
About the Future — 154
About Fruit — 155
About Giving — 157
About God — 158
About Good Works — 159
About Greatness — 160
About Heaven — 161
About Hell — 162
About Hypocrisy — 163
About Jerusalem — 164
About Judgment — 165
About the Kingdom — 167
About the Law — 169
About Love — 170
About Marriage — 171
About the Messiah — 173
About Miracles — 174
About Money — 176
About Neighbors — 177
About Oaths — 178
About Peace — 180
About Persecution — 180
About the Pharisees — 182
About the Poor — 183
About Prayer — 184
About Repentance — 185

About Rewards   187
About Resurrection   188
About the Sabbath   189
About Sacrifice   191
About Salvation   192
About Satan   193
About the Second Coming   194
About Service   195
About Sin   196
About Sinners   197
About Tradition   198
About the Trinity   199
About Works   201
About Worship   202

Appendices

Time for Review: What Jesus Does   205
My Favorite Life of Jesus Resources   209

Preface

After completing my college studies at the University of Oregon, I was privileged to attend Western Seminary where I completed my Master of Divinity and Master of Theology degrees. With graduation approaching, I was wondering what might be next on my academic horizon. Then, one afternoon I met a classmate walking across campus who greeted me and asked, "What are you going to do after graduation, swing into a doctoral program?"

"That's it," I thought to myself! I loved studying the Bible and had enjoyed each and every one of my classes at Western Seminary. But I wanted to go deeper into God's Word. And a doctoral program would provide that opportunity. With the blessing of my wife, who had already seen me through four years of seminary, I enrolled in a doctoral program at Dallas Theological Seminary.

Nancy and I spent the next three years living in Dallas, Texas, where we enjoyed southern hospitality, made great friends, and studied at Dallas Seminary. I was privileged to sit under the instruction of such men as Dr. Charles Ryrie, Dr. Donald Campbell, Dr. Elliot Johnson, Dr. Harold Hoehner, and my major professor, Dr. J. Dwight Pentecost. It was like being in heaven, studying with the angels and apostles! I completed my doctoral dissertation, "Selective Geographical Problems in the Life of Christ," in the summer of 1977 and began my teaching career at Western Seminary that fall.

Reflecting on my seven years of graduate studies at two great seminaries, there were many classes that enriched me spiritually and challenged me to think carefully about the message of the Bible. But one class stands out in my memory—the class I took from Dr.

Pentecost (affectionately known as *Dr. P*) on "the Life of Christ." During each class I scribbled on a yellow legal pad just about everything Dr. Pentecost said. Later in the day, I typed up those handwritten notes so I could read and study them later. In addition to listening to Dr. Pentecost's lectures that memorable semester, I was also reading Alfred Edersheim's classic book, "The Life and Times of Jesus the Messiah." My class notes, along with the insights gained from Edersheim's book, became the foundation of a class on the life of Christ I taught for many years at Western Seminary. It was my favorite class to teach and I am happy to say that my video lectures are still being used by Western Seminary students!

Since my retirement, I have contemplated writing a book on the life of Christ based on my years of teaching this subject. But there are many excellent books on the life of Christ. What might my book contribute to the subject?

While contemplating this question, I was asked to preach for two Sundays at a church where I had previously served as interim pastor. Since it was the Christmas season, I decided to preach two messages on the life of Christ. Wanting to do something that would solicit interest, my first sermon was "The Life of Christ *Before Birth*." My second message was titled "The Life of Christ *on Earth*." The messages were well received, but I realized there was more to the life of Christ than what I had presented in the two Christmas sermons. I decided that I needed to prepare another sermon on what Jesus is doing for us *now* in heaven ("The life of Christ *in Heaven*"). My fourth message would be about Jesus' plans for the future, "The life of Christ *in Prophecy*."

There are many lengthy and comprehensive books on the life of Christ, and I hope that you will read them. But this little book will focus on *essential* events (Part 1) and *key* teachings (Part 2) in the life of Christ. We won't just consider what Jesus did and taught during his life on earth. We will look back at what Jesus did *before* his birth in Bethlehem. Then, we will reflect on the key events in His earthly life as recorded in the four gospels. Following this survey, I will share some biblical texts that reveal what Jesus is doing *now* for us in heaven. Finally, in the last chapter we will consider the subject of biblical prophecy and discover what, according to Scripture, Jesus is going to do in the *future*.

My prayer is that this little book will help you get to know Jesus. And if you already know him in a personal way, I hope that as a result of reading this book, you will get to know Jesus *better!*

In his letter to the Philippian believers, the Apostle Paul wrote, "For me, to live is Christ" (Phil. 1:21). My prayer is that you will be more spiritually *alive* than ever before as you read and reflect on *The Story of Jesus*.

Part 1

What Jesus Does

Chapter 1

The Life of Christ Before Birth

Christmas is a special time of year. I love the smell of a fresh cut Christmas tree. I enjoy the colorful Christmas lights that brighten our neighborhood. I look forward with anticipation to Nancy's delicious cinnamon rolls which are served at breakfast on Christmas morning. Most of all, I enjoy the memories of past Christmases when all our family was together.

Christmas marks the beginning of the life of Christ on earth. But the birth of Jesus, which we celebrate at Christmas, wasn't actually the beginning of the life of Jesus. Although Jesus took on a human body when He was divinely conceived and began His earthly life in Bethlehem, He actually existed long *before* His physical birth!

John the Baptizer acknowledged this when he identified Jesus as the Lamb of God. John saw Jesus one day and said, "Behold, the lamb of God who takes away the sin of the world" (Jn. 1:29). Then he added, "This is the one of whom I said, 'After me comes a man who has a higher rank than I, for He existed before me.'"

Now to appreciate what John said, you must remember that John was about six months older than

Jesus (Lk. 1:36). Yet John declared that Jesus existed *before* he did! How can this be explained?

The only possible explanation is that the birth of Jesus was not the beginning of His actual existence. Jesus had a life and ministry before his physical birth! This is revealed as well in a conversation Jesus had with the religious leaders of ancient Israel. Jesus revealed both His deity and preexistence with the words, "Before Abraham was born, I Am" (John 8:58).

Careful study of the Bible reveals that there has *never* been a time in history when Jesus, the second person of the Trinity, did not exist. And that's what we want to consider as we begin our study of the life of Jesus. In this chapter we will consider the life of Christ *before* his birth.

The Bible makes it clear that God exists without a physical body. Jesus himself said, "God is spirit, and those who worship Him must worship in spirit and truth" (Jn. 4:24). Since He doesn't have a physical body, God cannot be seen with human eyes (Exod. 33:20; John 1:18; 5:37; 6:46, 1 Tim. 6:15-16). And yet there are situations in the Hebrew Bible where it is recorded that people "saw" God (Exod. 24:9-10; 33:23). How can this be? What did they see?

What they saw was God taking on a human-like body before Jesus took on humanity through His conception in Nazareth and birth in Bethlehem. Such an appearance of God in the Hebrew Bible is called a "theophany." This Greek word simply means "an appearance of God" and refers to a visible manifestation of a deity. Often these manifestations of God in the Hebrew Bible are referred to as "the Angel of the Lord" (Gen. 16:10-13; 22:11-15; 31:11, 32:28-30). From a Christian perspective, the appearances of God in the Old Testament are called "Christophanies" since they are actually appearances of *Jesus Christ* before His physical birth.

We should not be surprised that we can find Jesus revealed in the Old Testament. It was Jesus who said to the Jewish religious leaders, "You search the Scriptures because you think that in them you have eternal life; it is these that testify about me" (Jn. 5:39). After His resurrection, Jesus appeared and mildly rebuked two disciples walking on the road to Emmaus saying, "O foolish men and slow of heart to believe in all that the prophets have spoken! Was it not necessary for the Christ [Messiah] to suffer these things and to enter into His glory? And beginning with Moses and with all the prophets, He explained to them the things concerning Himself in all the Scriptures" (Lk. 24:25-27).

King David also spoke of the resurrection of Jesus in Psalm 16:8-11 when he prophesied that the Messiah would not be "abandoned" in the grave, nor would God the Father allow Him to "undergo decay" (Ps. 16:10). In his book, *The Messiah in the Old Testament*, Walt Kaiser has identified 65 direct predictions of the coming of Jesus in the Hebrew Bible.

So what was Jesus doing before his physical birth on earth? The Bible records at least twelve things Jesus did before His arrival as a baby in Bethlehem. Let's take a look at them.

Jesus Creating the Universe
Genesis 1, John 1, Colossians 1

You might not expect to find Jesus in the first verse of the Bible. But I believe He is there. Genesis 1:1 records,

"In the beginning God created the heavens and the earth." John the apostle recalls the work of creation in the very first verse of his gospel: "In the beginning was the Word, and the Word was with God, and the Word was God" (Jn. 1:1).

John goes on to offer his commentary on Genesis 1:1 with these words: "All things came into being through Him, and apart from Him nothing came into being that has come into being" (Jn. 1:3). The Apostle John is telling us that Jesus is the Creator of all things! And the Apostle Paul concurs. The first chapter of his letter to the Colossians is an exposition of the person and work of Jesus. In Colossians 1:16 he writes, "For by Him all things were created, both in the heavens and on earth, visible and invisible...all things have been created through Him and for Him."

The writer of Hebrews is another witness to the work of Jesus as Creator. He writes, "In these last days, God has spoken to us in His Son...through whom also He made the world" (Heb. 1:3).

Jesus was not only *present* at the very beginning of time, He is the One who *spoke* our universe into existence! As we consider the work of creation, I believe that each person of the Trinity had an active part. God the Father was the designer and architect of creation. God the Son was the agent of creation. He spoke creation into existence. And God the Holy Spirit was there too, "moving over" or "hovering over" creation in a protective manner (Gen. 1:3). There is just one Creator God, but His work of creation was accomplished through the participation and interaction of the three co-equal persons of the Trinity. While this can be a bit mind-boggling, the important thing to remember is that Jesus is the creator of our physical universe. To know him is to know the Creator!

Jesus Visiting with Abraham
Genesis 18

Jesus appears again in the pages of the Bible where we find Him visiting Abraham, the great patriarch of the Hebrew people. Abraham was sitting in front of his tent one day when three men approached. Following the custom of the Ancient Near East, Abraham welcomed the visitors and insisted on preparing them a meal. One of the men is identified in the biblical text as "the Lord" (Gen. 18:13). This is a reference to the Angel of the Lord, the divine person we know in the New Testament as Jesus.

That day, the Lord revealed two future events to Abraham. First, the aged Sarah was going to have a son (Gen. 18:10). Second, the wicked city of Sodom was going to be destroyed (Gen. 18:16-33). This intriguing conversation with Abraham reveals that Jesus knows the future (Matt. 16:21) and that He is the ultimate judge (Jn. 5:27-30).

But we also see the fairness and mercy of Jesus in this text. In response to the appeal of Abraham, Jesus promises to spare Sodom from judgment if he finds ten righteous men there (Gen. 18:32). But, as we know, the numbers didn't add up. And the city of Sodom was destroyed. Sadly, only Lot and his two daughters survived God's judgment on Sodom. Lot's wife looked back, disobeying the angels' instructions, and "became a pillar of salt" (Gen. 19:17,26).

17

Jesus Wrestling with Jacob
Genesis 32

Our next encounter with Jesus in the pages of the Hebrew Bible is in Genesis 32 where Jesus wrestled with Jacob. It is helpful for us to understand the background of this encounter. You may recall that Esau had sold his birthright to his younger twin brother, Jacob. Then, Jacob had tricked his father, Isaac, into bestowing on him the patriarchal blessing. Esau was so angry about this that he was planning to kill Jacob. So Jacob fled from the land of Canaan and went to live with his uncle, Laban, for about 20 years Gen. 27-28).

During his time away from home, Jacob married Leah and Rachel and raised a family. But when his relationship with Uncle Laban deteriorated, Jacob was instructed by the Lord to leave Paddan-Aram and return home (Gen. 31:1-3). He was approaching the borders of the Promised Land when he learned that Esau was coming to meet him—with an army of 400 men (Gen. 32:6)! The Bible reports that Jacob was "greatly afraid and distressed," believing that he was going to be attacked and punished by his brother (Gen. 32:7).

That night as Jacob camped on the banks of the Jabbok River, a strange man approached him and a wrestling match ensued. All night long Jacob wrestled with this stranger. As dawn was breaking, the man said, "Let me go, for the dawn is breaking!" And Jacob replied, "I will not let you go unless you bless me!" (Gen. 32:26).

When the wrestling match was over and the stranger departed, Jacob named the place "Peniel" meaning "face of God," adding, "I have seen God face to face" (Gen. 32:30). Jacob's words reveal the identity of the stranger, indicating that this is another encounter with Jesus before His incarnation.

Jacob's fears over meeting his brother Esau were relieved by his encounter with Jesus who blessed him and gave him a new name, "Israel," along with a confident attitude. He would no longer be known as "Jacob the *usurper.*" By his new name, he would be known as "Israel, the *victor.*"

Jesus leading Israel Through the Wilderness
Exodus 23

When the Israelites arrived at Mt. Sinai after the exodus from Egypt, they entered into a covenant with God. The covenant God had made with Abraham was *unconditional*. God simply promised that He would make Abraham into a great nation, that He would give Abraham's descendants a land, and that He would bless Abraham and through him bring blessing to the whole world (Gen. 12:2-3). There were no reciprocal actions required of Abraham in order for the promises of the covenant to be fulfilled. The covenant God made with the people of Israel at Mt. Sinai was different. It was a *conditional* covenant. God promised his people Israel that they would experience blessing in the promised land when they obeyed the stipulations of the covenant. In the covenant made at Mt. Sinai, the blessings were conditioned on obedience. No obedience—no blessing (Deut.28:1-6).

It was in the context of revealing and explaining the covenant stipulations that God made a promise which would encourage and sustain His people through their

19

long and hazardous wilderness experience. God told Moses, "Behold, I am going to send an angel to guard you along the way and to bring you into the place which I have prepared" (Exod. 23:20). The "angel" God was sending to guard and guide Israel was not simply a passenger on the bus. God explained that "My name is in him" (Gen. 23:21). This statement is a clue as to the identity of the angel. He is so closely identified with God that he bears God's name! The relationship between God and Israel's protecting angel is further evidenced by the words of verse 22. God told Moses and the people of Israel that they must "obey his voice and do all that I say (Exod. 23:22). The voice of the angel was the voice of God!

Who was this angel that guarded and guided God's people during their 40-year wilderness journey from Egypt to Canaan? I believe it is none other than the Angel of the Lord, the pre-incarnate Jesus! God didn't leave his people alone in the wilderness of Sinai to fend for themselves against their adversaries. God promised Israel to be "an enemy to your enemies and an adversary to your adversaries" (Exod. 23:22). God's angel, the Lord Jesus, would go before Israel, defending them from their enemies, and bringing them safely into their promised land (Exod. 23:23).

How comforting it is to know that Jesus is always on the job! Jesus continues to guide His people through their wilderness experiences and defend them from attacks by their spiritual enemies! The power and presence of Jesus enabled the Israelites to enter their promised land. And we can be confident that Jesus who said, "I am with you always" (Matt. 28:20), is with us today, guiding and protecting as we journey through life and on to heaven.

Jesus Revealing Himself to Moses
Exodus 34

One of the most amazing appearances of Jesus in the Hebrew Bible is found in Exodus 34, where Jesus revealed himself to Moses. This event in the life of Christ took place at the foot of Mt. Sinai about 1400 years before His birth!

The people of Israel had entered into a covenant with God at Mt. Sinai. They had agreed to the stipulations of the covenant and had promised to worship and serve God alone (Exod. 19:5-8; 24:3-8). But while Moses was up on Mt. Sinai receiving further instructions from the Lord, the Israelites became anxious and asked Aaron to make them a god they could see and follow (Exod. 32:1).

Aaron took some gold and fashioned a golden calf which he introduced to the people with the words, "This is your god, O Israel, who brought you up from the land of Egypt" (Exod. 32:4). The people had broken the first of God's commandments, "You shall have no other gods before Me" (Exod. 20:3).

What was Moses to do? Disappointed and discouraged, he returned to Mt. Sinai asking God for a fresh vision of His glory (33:18). God answered and said, "You can't see my face, for no man can see me and live. But I will put you in the cleft of a rock and cover you with my hand until I have passed by. Then I will take My hand away and you shall see My back, but My face shall not be seen" (Exod. 33:20-23).

Then the Lord descended in a cloud onto Mt. Sinai and passed by in front of Moses. After God passed by declaring, "The Lord, the Lord God," He removed His hand and Moses saw God's back.

This is powerful language! It speaks of an intimate and very close encounter with the living God! Whose "back" did Moses see? Since God is spirit and doesn't have a physical "back," this must have been an appearance of Jesus. Moses saw the back of Jesus nearly a millennia-and-a-half before Joseph and Mary saw His face as a baby born in Bethlehem. The experience of seeing Jesus' back had a powerful impact on Moses. The skin on his face actually *shone* because of his encounter with Jesus (Exod. 34:29-30). How much more should the personal presence of Jesus impact the lives of His followers today!

Jesus Commanding Joshua
Joshua 5

In the book which bears his name, we read of how Joshua was commissioned to lead Israel's army in the conquest of Canaan. Joshua was commander of the Israelite army. But just after crossing the Jordan River into the Promised Land, Joshua had an encounter which revealed that while he was the commander, he wasn't Israel's commander-in-chief!

Joshua was near the city of Jericho when he saw a man standing opposite him with his sword drawn. Was this an enemy threatening Israel's leader? Puzzled, Joshua asked him, "Are you for us or for our adversaries?" (Josh. 5:13).

The answer brought Joshua to his knees. The visitor responded, "No, rather I come now as *captain* of the host of the Lord" (Josh. 5:14). Joshua quickly realized that the visitor only *appeared* to be human! He responded with respect and submission, "What has my Lord to say to His servant" (Josh. 5:14)?

The answer given by Israel's Captain is reminiscent of Moses' encounter with God at the burning bush. God said, "Remove your sandals from your feet, for the place where you are standing is holy" (Josh. 5:15). As God had revealed Himself to Moses at Mt. Sinai, so He was doing the same with Joshua. Joshua would lead Israel. But Jesus would lead Joshua!

This encounter with the pre-incarnate Jesus must have been a great encouragement to Joshua as he prepared for the battle at Jericho. It was encouraging to know that he was not alone in leading Israel in the conquest of Canaan. Jesus was with Joshua, just as He is with you and me today (Matt. 28:20).

Jesus Encouraging Gideon
Judges 6

In Judges 6 we read of how the Midianites were invading the land and stealing Israel's crops. The people were desperate for someone who could lead them in victory over the invaders.

One day as Gideon was trying to salvage some wheat from the Midianite raiders, the Angel of the Lord appeared to him and said, "Go in your strength and deliver Israel from the hand of Midian. Have I not sent you?" (Judg. 6:14).

At first Gideon wasn't sure of the identity of this visitor. "Was it really the Lord? Could his words be

23

trusted?" So Gideon asked for a sign. "Show me a sign that it is You who speaks with me" (Judg. 6:17).

The Angel of the Lord instructed Joshua to prepare a sacrifice and place it on a rock. Then the angel touched the offering with his staff and fire "sprang up from the rock, consuming the meat and bread" (Judg. 6:21).

Gideon suddenly understood that he was face to face with God! He exclaimed, "Alas, O Lord GOD! For I have seen the Angel of the Lord face to face" (Judg. 6:22). To commemorate his personal encounter with the living God, Gideon built an altar and named it "Yahweh Shalom," (Yahweh is peace). Jesus would later tell his disciples, "Peace I leave with you; My peace I give to you" (Jn. 14:27). With this encouragement from Jesus, who "is our peace" (Eph. 2:14), Gideon went on to lead Israel in a great victory over the Midianites.

Jesus Announcing Samson's Birth
Judges 13

Jesus appears again in the book of Judges when "the Angel of the LORD" appeared to a barren woman announcing that she would have a son (Judg. 13:3). She was also instructed not to drink wine or eat anything unclean, for her son would be a Nazirite from birth (Judg. 13:5). When relating the encounter to her husband, Manoah, she described the messenger saying, "A man of God came to me and his appearance was like the appearance of the angel of God, very awesome" (Judg. 13:6). Although Manoah might have been a bit skeptical over the announcement that his barren wife would conceive and give birth to a son, he didn't show it in his response. Embracing the revelation by faith, he prayed that God would send the messenger again to instruct him "what to do for the boy who is to be born" (Judg. 13:8).

In response to His prayer for clarity, the Angel of the Lord appeared again. This time he explained to Manoah, as he had to his wife, that their son would be Nazirite from birth. So during the pregnancy, Manoah's wife "should not eat anything that comes from the vine nor drink wine or strong drink, nor eat any unclean thing" (Judg. 13:14; cf. Num. 6:1-21).

Like Gideon, Manoah prepared a sacrifice to honor the visitor. When fire sprang up from the altar, Manoah realized that he and his wife had *seen* God and would most certainly die! (Judg. 13:22). But they didn't die. Instead, they had a baby, just as the Lord promised. And they named him Samson. Although Samson's mother appears to have kept the Nazirite requirements during her pregnancy, sadly her son didn't during his lifetime. Parenting can be a great joy. But children who turn from God and His Word can also be a source of disappointment.

Jesus Calling Isaiah to Ministry
Isaiah 6

At the beginning of his ministry, the prophet Isaiah had an amazing vision which is recorded for us in Isaiah 6:1-4. Seeing the Lord in all his holiness, Isaiah saw himself in all his sin.

Isaiah cried out, "Woe is me, for I am ruined, because I am a man of unclean lips...for my eyes have seen the King, the Lord of Hosts!" (Isa. 6:5). In response to his confession of sin, one of the angelic creatures flew to Isaiah with a burning coal and touched his lips with it. The angel then announced, "Your iniquity is taken away and your sin is forgiven (Isa. 6:7)."

Then the Lord asked, "Whom shall I send, and who will go for us?" (Isa. 6:8).

Isaiah responded, "Here I am. Send me!"

The apostle John refers to Isaiah's call in chapter 12 of his gospel. He records how the ministry of Jesus fulfilled the words of Isaiah the prophet. Then John adds these words: "These things Isaiah said because He saw His glory and spoke of Him" (Jn. 12:41).

Who was John referring to? It is clear from the context that he is referring to Jesus. The Apostle John is telling us that the Lord of Hosts, whom Isaiah saw on a throne in the temple, was none other than Jesus! Isaiah saw the glory of the pre-incarnate Jesus and recorded it in his prophecy. Isaiah, whose writings tell us so much prophetically about the person and work of the Messiah, was privileged to *see* the Promised One before his birth!

Jesus Comforting Daniel's Friends
Daniel 3

One of my favorite stories in the Bible is the account of Daniel's three friends in the fiery furnace. King Nebuchadnezzar had made a golden image and set it up for all the people of Babylon to worship. They were told, "When you hear the music, you are to fall down and worship the golden image. And whoever does not fall down and worship shall immediately be cast into the midst of a furnace of blazing fire" (Dan. 3:5-6).

26

What could Shadrach, Meshach and Abednego do? Would they compromise to save their lives? Would they kneel down and worship the golden image? What would *you* do if faced with a similar situation?

When music began to play, everyone gathered around Nebuchadnezzar's golden image and fell down before the image to worship—everyone except Shadrach, Meshach and Abednego. For their refusal to worship, they were hauled before king Nebuchadnezzar. Perhaps there was a misunderstanding. The king offered them another chance. Giving them the benefit of the doubt, the king allowed for the possibility that the men didn't understand. He would be glad to give them another chance. He reviewed the requirement and then warned, "But if you do not worship, you will immediately be cast into the midst of a furnace of blazing fire; and what god is there who can deliver you out of my hands?" (Dan. 3:15).

It was a life threatening situation. To worship meant life. To disobey meant death. What would they do? Would they compromise God's law to save their lives? Daniel's friends replied, "Our God whom we serve is able to deliver us from the furnace of blazing fire…but even if He does not, we are not going to worship your gods or the golden image that you have set up" (Dan. 3:17-18). For Daniel's friends, obeying God was more important than saving their lives.

Well, you know the story. Into the fiery furnace they went! The fact that the inferno was HOT is evidenced by the deaths of the men who cast Daniel's friends into the furnace (Dan. 3:22). Then, as Nebuchadnezzar gazed into the fiery furnace, he was shocked to see not three men, but four! And they were not burning like toast, but were walking about with no apparent harm from the flames! What was happening? And who was that fourth person?

As he witnessed the obvious miracle, King Nebuchadnezzar exclaimed that the fourth figure had the "appearance of a son of the gods." And he was right! The fourth person in the fiery furnace was another appearance of the Angel of the Lord. Jesus had taken on human form and had entered the fiery furnace to comfort and encourage Daniel's courageous friends.

What a story Daniel's three friends were able to share with their children and grandchildren! I can just imagine that years later their grandchildren would say, "Tell us again, gramps, about how you were in the fiery furnace walking and talking with God!" I trust that none of my readers will ever face the flames of martyrdom; but if that occasion should arise, the courage and commitment of Shadrach, Meshach and Abednego has given us an example to follow.

Jesus Shutting the Lions' Mouths
Daniel 6

There is considerable debate as to which is the most exciting story of the Bible. Is it the story David and Goliath, Daniel's friends in the fiery furnace, or Jonah being swallowed by the big fish? Whatever your ranking, the event recorded in Daniel 6 has to be in your top ten. It records one of the most familiar stories of the Bible, revealing Daniel's priorities and personal commitment to serving and obeying God.

Daniel held a high position of authority in the Persian government under King Darius. But his subordinates were jealous that a Judean (Jew) should be in such a high and

28

honored position. This reflects an attitude of anti-Semitism—hatred and hostility against Jewish people. The commissioners under Daniel looked for grounds to accuse him. But his personal and professional life were above reproach. So the commissioners devised an evil plan to create a conflict between Daniel's personal, spiritual life and Persian governmental regulations. The leaders of this conspiracy petitioned King Darius for a thirty-day ban on prayer. During this period, the people of Persia would be forbidden to pray. The royal injunction included a penalty for disobedience. "Anyone who makes a petition to any god or man besides you, O King, shall be cast into the lions' den" (Dan. 6:7). Daniel's enemies knew that he was in the habit of praying three times a day. It would be easy to catch and accuse Daniel of violating the king's decree.

Daniel was committed to serving God—even when there was a price to be paid. Faithful in his pattern of prayer, Daniel was accused of violating the royal decree. His accusers reported to Darius, "Daniel, who is one of the exiles from Judah, pays no attention to you, O King, or to the injunction which you signed, but keeps making his petition three times a day" (Dan. 6:13). Although Darius wanted to spare Daniel's life, he was trapped by his own legislation. The laws of the Medes and Persians were inviable. Once enacted, they could not be changed—even by the king! So Daniel was taken from the king's court and thrown into a pit filled with hungry lions. From a human perspective, it appeared to be the end of Daniel's career—and his life!

But God had other plans for Daniel. Instead of pouncing on Daniel to make a quick meal of him, the lions discovered that their huge jaws were clamped shut by some invisible force. They must have concluded that there was no point in pouncing on their victim if they couldn't eat him! Daniel spent the night in the pit with the hungry lions. He woke up the next morning with all his arms and legs still attached. Daniel was totally unharmed by the fierce and hungry lions!

King Darius, who had spent the night in prayer for Daniel (Dan. 6:18), came to the pit early the next morning to see if Daniel had survived. "Daniel, was the God whom you serve so loyally able to save you from the lions?" (Dan. 6:19). Daniel responded, "My God sent His angel and shut the lions' mouths and they have not harmed me, in as much as I was found innocent before Him; and also toward you, O King, I have committed no crime" (Dan. 6:22). Who was this "angel" who shut the mouths of the lions? The word translated "angel" literally means "messenger." The messenger could have been Michael or Gabriel or some other unnamed angelic messenger. But I suggest another possibility. I believe that the one who shut the lions' mouths was the same unnamed figure who was present with Daniel's friends in the fiery furnace; someone described as having the appearance of "a son of the gods" (Dan. 3: 25). What we have in the lions' den is another appearance of Jesus before His birth in Bethlehem. As Jesus was with Daniel's friends in a time of severe testing, so He was with Daniel.

God's deliverance of Daniel does not mean that this is always His will. God delivered Peter and Paul, but not Stephen or James. Peter and Paul were delivered from prison and had an extended ministry. Stephen and James faced death and had an early promotion to heaven. But it is comforting to know that Jesus *can* shut the mouths of lions! And He promises to be with us when we encounter life's most severe and challenging trials (Matt. 28:20).

Jesus Cleansing Israel's High Priest
Zechariah 3

The last appearance of Jesus in the Hebrew Bible is found in the book of Zechariah. Zechariah was a prophet who ministered to the Judean people after their return from Babylon. The people returned to a burned out city and a destroyed temple. The sin that led to the Babylonian exile still weighed heavily on their consciences. In Zechariah 3 we read of an encounter between Israel's high priest, the Angel of the Lord, and Satan, the "accuser of the brethren" (Rev. 12:10). The cast in this mini-drama is presented as follows:

The *high priest* (representing Israel) is Joshua.
The *Angel of the Lord* is Jesus, God in human form.
The *accuser* is Satan (Hebrew for "accuser" or "slanderer").

Joshua, the high priest, was standing in filthy garments before the Lord God. The soiled garments are a picture of the sinful condition of the people and their priest. God's enemy, Satan, was standing to the right of the Angel of the Lord accusing Joshua, Israel's high priest, of sin.

Then God commanded those standing by, "Remove the filthy garments from him" (Zech. 3:4). After the garments were removed, God Himself explained the significance. "See, I have taken your iniquity from you and will clothe you with festal robes" (Zech. 3:4). So they put a clean turban on Joshua's head and clothed him with clean, white garments as the Angel of the Lord—that is Jesus—was standing by.

The removal and replacement of Joshua's filthy garments is a picture of what happens to believers when they place their trust in Jesus. When we believe in Jesus as our sin-bearing Savior, our iniquity is removed and replaced with the righteousness of Christ. Jesus takes our sin upon Himself and freely bestows on us His own righteousness. This is a wonderful truth that is further developed by the Apostle Paul in Romans 3-5 and captured concisely in 2 Corinthians 5:21, "He made Him who knew no sin to be sin on our behalf, so that we might become the righteousness of God in Him." Jesus took our sin and gave us His righteousness. This truth of amazing grace was foretold long ago by the cleansing of Joshua, Israel's high priest.

Conclusion

We have been considering the life and ministry of Jesus before His birth in Bethlehem. This is not just academic information. The kinds of things that Jesus did before His birth are the kinds of ministries He is performing now.

➢ Although His work of creation is complete, Jesus continues to sustain creation.
➢ He continues to seek out His people, as He did Abraham.
➢ He continues to reveal Himself to those who love Him, as He did with Moses.

- ➢ He continues to lead and command His followers, as he did with Joshua.
- ➢ He continues to encourage fearful people, as He did with Jacob and Gideon.
- ➢ He continues to call men and women to serve Him, as he did with Isaiah.
- ➢ He continues to be with us in times of trial, as He was with Daniel and his three friends.
- ➢ And Jesus continues to cleanse repentant people from their sin and iniquity and grant them His righteousness.

Jesus is willing to do all this for you if you are willing to invite Him into your life. Hebrews 11:6 says, "And without faith it is impossible to please Him, for he who comes to God must believe that He is and that He is a rewarder of those who seek Him."

If you are seeking God, Jesus the Good Shepherd, is going to find you! And when you become one of His own children, He will do for *you* what He has been doing for His people for all eternity. I invite you to receive God's greatest gift—salvation through God's Promised One, Jesus.

Chapter 2

The Life of Jesus on Earth

For many of us, Christmas is our favorite time of year. We enjoy the Christmas lights, the smell of a fresh cut Christmas tree, delicious holiday food, and the memories we have of this special time of year.

What is troubling about the Christmas season these days is that the true meaning of Christmas is often lost in the busy schedule of fun and festivities. Yes, we light advent candles and arrange our nativity displays; and that's all good. But after the holiday season has passed and the tree is recycled or put into a box, what do we really remember about the life of Jesus on earth?

Many books have been written on the life of Christ. Readers often get overwhelmed by the many stories, parables and miracles which are so important in the life of Christ. In this chapter, I am going to focus on twenty-four *key events* of the life of Jesus on earth. We will use the Gospel of Matthew as the main text for our study.

Jesus' Virgin Birth
Matthew 1:16-25

The birth of Jesus is *the* most significant event in human history. In fact, history is divided by His birth—B.C. [before Christ] and A.D. [*Anno Domini*, in the year of our Lord]. The most unusual thing about the birth of Jesus is that He was born of a virgin, without a human father. Matthew records that before Joseph and Mary had come together as a married couple, Mary was found to be pregnant (Matt. 1:18). Many scholars and critics view the virgin birth as no more possible than turning the Nile River into blood, parting the Red Sea, raising Lazarus or walking on water. Miracles just don't happen and miracle stories must be dismissed or explained as the result of natural events. The fact is biblical miracles can't be explained by the natural world. We must either accept these supernatural works of God by faith or reject the message of the Bible.

How would you respond if you discovered that the woman you were planning to marry was pregnant? Can you imagine the shock and disappointment Joseph must have experienced?

There were two avenues open to Joseph: (1) public lawsuit or (2) quiet separation. Joseph, being a righteous man and not wanting to shame Mary and further embarrass her family, chose to end their relationship quietly (Matt. 1:19). But while Joseph was contemplating this course of action, an angel met him and explained that Mary's pregnancy was not the result of an illicit affair, but that the child that had been conceived was "of the Holy Spirit" (Matt. 1:20; Lk. 1:35-38).

The angel also gave the baby His name—Yeshua (Matt. 1:21). The name, usually pronounced "Jesus," means "salvation." The name reveals what Jesus came to do. He came to earth to be the means of salvation for all who would welcome Him and receive the gift of His saving work.

Matthew wants us to know that the virgin birth of Jesus took place in fulfillment of prophecy (Matt. 1:22-23). Isaiah 7:14 is the first in a long list of prophecies designed to demonstrate that Jesus is Israel's long awaited Messiah. Although Joseph took Mary as his wife immediately after receiving the angel's message, he kept her as a virgin until she had given birth to Jesus (Matt. 1:24-25).

The birth of Jesus fulfilled another prophecy as well—Micah 5:2. Seven hundred years before Jesus was born, the prophet Micah announced that the promised Messiah would be born not in Nazareth, Joseph and Mary's home village, but in the little town of Bethlehem. This is significant because King David was from Bethlehem. And Jesus came in fulfillment of the promise that David would have a son who would sit on his throne and rule forever (2 Sam. 7:16). Matthew's genealogy demonstrates the genealogical link between King David and Jesus (Matt. 1:1-17). The virgin birth of Jesus in the town of Bethlehem serves as proof that He was the long awaited messianic descendant of David!

Jesus' Early Years in Nazareth
Matthew 2:23

After a brief sojourn in Egypt to avoid the death threat against Jesus by wicked King Herod, Joseph led his little family back to his home in Nazareth. It was here in this small and insignificant village situated in lower Galilee that Jesus grew up (Matt. 2:23, Lk. 2:51, 4:16).

We know very little about the first thirty years of Jesus earthly life. The gospels of Matthew and Luke record His birth. Mark and John begin their gospel accounts with Jesus being introduced as an adult by John the Baptizer. But what happened in between?

It was during these silent years that Jesus was quietly being prepared for His lifetime work. Although Nazareth was a small village, with a population of perhaps several hundred, it was not completely isolated from the Roman world. Just four miles to the north was Sepphoris, the Roman capital of Galilee. Lots of building was going on there, and since Joseph was a "builder" (*teknon*, Matt. 13:55), it is likely that he would have found work at a growing city so close to Nazareth. Since it was the responsibility of a Jewish father to teach his son a trade, it is likely that Jesus would have worked at Sepphoris as an apprentice with Joseph. Working at the regional capital of Galilee, Jesus would have been exposed to the broader Roman world and culture.

Just to the south of Nazareth was a rocky outcrop overlooking the Jezreel Valley where Jesus and His friends might have looked down on the travelers and caravans journeying across the broad valley between the regions north and south of Israel. Perhaps this exposure to the surrounding Roman world was preparing Jesus for his ministry to the nations.

While the *bar mitzvah* ceremony wasn't practiced formally before the sixth century A.D., Jesus would have received spiritual instruction in the home from His godly mother, Mary. He would have also received instruction in the Torah from the local synagogue. Luke records a situation when Jesus, at the age of twelve, was visiting Jerusalem with his family for Passover (Lk. 2:41-50). Today's parents are somewhat shocked to read about Jesus being inadvertently left behind when Joseph and Mary began their journey back to Nazareth. When Joseph and Mary discovered that Jesus was not with the caravan of travelers returning to Galilee, they retraced their steps to Jerusalem to search for their young son. Luke records that "they found him in the temple, sitting in the midst of the teachers, both listening to them and asking them questions" (Lk. 2:46). Even at a young age, Jesus demonstrated an impressive understanding of God and His Word. Luke adds the telling observation, "And all who heard Him were amazed at His understanding and His answers" (Lk. 2:47).

The paucity of information about the early life of Jesus leaves us with many questions. When did the child Jesus know that He was God? When did He become aware of His messianic mission? Was Jesus, as a child, capable of using His miraculous powers? Although we would like to know more about the early years of Jesus as a child and as a young man, such information is not essential to the story of His life and ministry. Yet Luke tells us that during these early years Jesus "continued in subjection" to His parents as He was growing and maturing (Lk. 2:50). Luke adds that Jesus "kept increasing in wisdom and stature, and in favor with God and men" (Lk. 2:51).

Jesus' Approval at His Baptism
Matthew 3:13-17

Jesus was about thirty years old when He was baptized in the Jordan River near the place where the Israelites crossed the Jordan into Canaan. The word "baptize" is actually a Greek word that has been left *untranslated* in our Bibles. The word simply means "to immerse" in water. The word is used of people who drown and ships that sink. Immersion in water for the purpose of ritual purification was a very common practice in Judaism. But Jesus didn't have any sin and so there was no need for ritual cleansing. Why, then, did Jesus go to John for baptism (Matt. 3:14)? Why did He need to be immersed?

Matthew explains three reasons why Jesus was immersed. *First*, it was done "to fulfill all righteousness" (Matt. 3:15). "Righteousness" refers to what is right. John the Baptizer at first objected to baptizing Jesus. Then he consented, knowing that it was God's will and therefore the "right" thing to do.

Second, Jesus was immersed to receive empowerment through the ministry of the Holy Spirit (Matt. 3:16). Several Jewish writings refer to the "dove" as a symbol of the Holy Spirit. Jesus was already divine at His birth. He didn't take on deity at His baptism. But at Jesus' baptism He received a special anointing by the Holy Spirit, empowering Him to carry on His earthly ministry (Acts 10:38).

The *third* reason for Jesus' immersion in water was that it provided an opportunity for God to declare His acceptance and approval of His Son. When Jesus came up out of the water, a voice from heaven declared, "This is my beloved Son, in whom I am well pleased" (Matt. 3:17). This is the first of three times that God spoke from heaven to identify and affirm Jesus as His Son. The voice from heaven was heard again at Jesus' transfiguration (Matt. 17:5) and following His royal entry into Jerusalem (Jn. 12:28).

The baptism of Jesus also served to identify Him with John the Baptizer and John's fledgling messianic movement. John then presented Jesus to the people of Israel with his words, "Behold, the Lamb of God who takes away the sin of the world" (Jn. 1:29). Jesus' baptism was the official initiation and introduction into His public, messianic ministry.

Jesus' Testing Through Temptation
Matthew 4:1-11

Shortly after His immersion in the Jordan River, Jesus was "led by the Spirit into the wilderness to be tempted by the devil" (Matt. 4:1). Matthew reports that the temptation of Jesus was initiated by the Holy Spirit, but orchestrated by God's enemy, Satan. It appears that God's purpose in the temptation was to demonstrate the sinlessness of Jesus through His obedience to the Father's will. Satan, on the other hand, wanted to make Jesus sin by taking shortcuts to the accomplishment of His messianic purposes. God's good purpose and Satan's evil design coalesced at Jesus' temptation.

41

In His first temptation (Matt. 4:3-4), Jesus was encouraged to turn the stones of the wilderness into bread. Jesus had been fasting for forty days and nights, and was no doubt very hungry. Fasting is an expression of dependence on God for spiritual strength and energy. Satan was saying, "Stop trusting in God to meet your needs. Use your own power to satisfy your hunger." Jesus refused this temptation, quoting from Deut. 8:3, "Man shall not live on bread alone, but on every word that proceeds out of the mouth of God" (Matt. 4:4). Jesus was saying that God's Word of truth is more important in life than physical food. Eat mere food and you will eventually die! Feed on the truth of God's Word and you will live forever.

At His second temptation (Matt. 4:5-7), Jesus was challenged to throw Himself off the pinnacle of Jerusalem's temple. The "pinnacle" probably refers to the southwest corner tower located just above the busy intersection of the north-south and east-west streets of Jerusalem. To witness Jesus leaping from the temple tower and being caught by angels would have been a great publicity stunt and would have attracted a lot of attention for Jesus. But it would also be testing God to protect Him from harm. Jesus refused the temptation to test God's faithfulness. He knew that you don't need to test someone you genuinely trust.

The third temptation of Jesus (Matt. 4:8-11) may have been the most difficult. As Israel's Messiah, Jesus came to earth to receive His kingdom (Matt. 4:17). But He must have known that His kingdom offer would be ultimately rejected. In the third temptation, Satan offered Jesus all

42

the kingdoms of the world if Jesus would simply bow down before him. It was the offer of an easy path to the Davidic throne! No cross; no suffering; no death. Satan was saying, "*You can have your promised earthly kingdom with one little bow of the knee!*" But Jesus refused the offer. He refused to bow down before Satan. There is only One who is worthy of worship—our heavenly Father.

It is significant that each time Jesus was tempted, He appealed to Scripture to demonstrate that what Satan was asking Him to do was contrary to God's revealed will. The temptation of Jesus sets Him forth as the perfect Son of God who was perfectly qualified to redeem humanity and rule heaven and earth. Jesus' response to Satan's temptation settles once and for all the question of His sinlessness. As the sinless Savior of sinful humanity, Jesus is perfectly qualified to take His promised throne and rule the nations of the earth.

Jesus' Offer of the Kingdom
Matthew 4:17

Jesus launched His public preaching ministry in Galilee with the words, "Repent, the kingdom of heaven is at hand" (Matt. 4:17). What did He mean by "repent"? How did His listeners understand Jesus' announcement that "the kingdom of heaven is at hand?".

The word "repent" literally means to "turn around," and suggests the idea of a change of mind. A change of mind leads to a change of direction. So what did Jesus mean by telling people to "repent?" What did Jesus want people to repent of?

Jesus was telling those who would listen, "Don't be deceived. Being Jewish doesn't mean that you will have a place in God's kingdom. You need a fresh start! You need to turn your spiritual life around and go in a different direction. You must be born again!" This was Jesus' message for the Jewish teacher Nicodemus who came with his questions at night (Jn. 3:3).

The Jewish people in Jesus' day thought that being Jewish was sufficient to guarantee a bright and eternal future. It was believed by many Jews that their good works and righteous actions would earn them a place in God's future kingdom. Jesus was saying, "Repent of these wrong views! Good works should accompany salvation, but they can't save you. Find your salvation in Me!"

In addition to calling Jewish people to repentance, Jesus was announcing "The kingdom of heaven is at hand." (Matt. 4:17). In parallel passages, Jesus uses the expression, "kingdom of God." Out of respect for Jewish sensitivities and tradition in referring of God, Matthew substitutes the expression "kingdom of heaven." It appears clear that that "kingdom of heaven" and "kingdom of God" are equivalent expressions.

Much has been written about what Jesus meant by "the kingdom of God." I suggest that the kingdom of God has three main features—people, place and rule. The kingdom of God may be described quite simply as "God's people, in God's place, under God's rule." The kingdom of

God is a present spiritual reality that will be ultimately realized in physical form.

The prophets told the people of Israel that the kingdom would be a time of peace, prosperity, justice and good health (Isa. 35:5-6). You can imagine how the people of Israel longed for the coming of God's kingdom. They looked forward with great anticipation to this time of blessing. Before Jesus was born, the angel Gabriel told Mary that her son was destined to receive the throne of David and rule God's kingdom forever (Lk. 1:31-33).

John the Baptizer had announced the coming of King Jesus. Now, Jesus had arrived on the scene. And He was announcing to the people of Israel, "The prophesied kingdom is available for you now! Repent of your wrong views and accept Me as your true, messianic king!"

Jesus' Authentication by Miracles
Matthew 4:23

We are studying the life of a man who claimed to be God. He claimed to be the promised Messiah whom the Jews had long anticipated. He came offering the kingdom to those who would receive Him by faith. He claimed to be the only way to God. But many people were understandably skeptical.

What would it take to convince them that Jesus' claims were valid? He didn't carry any official documents to prove His messianic authority. But Jesus did present credentials intended to authenticate Him as God's Son and Israel's Messiah. Jesus' official credentials were His miracles.

The miracles of Jesus were not intended to merely gain attention or get a following. The miracles of Jesus served to authenticate that He was the Son of God and brought God's message of salvation to the people of Israel. Jesus' preaching was usually followed by a miracle (Matt. 4:23). Jesus authenticated the truth of His Sermon on the Mount by healing a leper (Matt. 8:1-4). He authenticated His claim to be the "light of the world" by giving sight to the man born blind (Jn. 8:12; 9:1-7). Jesus' miraculous works served to validate the truth of His words.

Jesus' first miracle took place in Cana of Galilee where He provided for the wedding guests by changing water into wine (Jn. 2:1-11). His last earthly miracle provided a memorable catch of *large* fish (153 to be exact) for the fishermen He had called as apostles (Jn. 21:1-11). There are thirty-six specifically recorded miracles of Jesus in the four gospels. Many others are referred to more generally (Matt. 4:23; Lk. 7:21-22). The miracles demonstrate that Jesus is who He claimed to be—Israel's Messiah, the Son of God.

The main word used by the gospel writers to refer to Jesus' miracles is "sign" (*semeion*). You could say that the miracles of Jesus were *signposts* pointing to His deity and messiahship. Jesus most often refers to His miracles as His "works" (*ergon*). The miracles are the divine works of God. Another word used of Jesus' miracles is "wonders" (*teras*), alluding to the wonder and amazement in the minds of those who witnessed His miracles.

In addition to authenticating Jesus' messiahship and kingdom message, the miracles served three other purposes. First, the miracles were tools of instruction for His disciples. The miracles taught of Jesus' power (Mk. 5:1-20), provision (Jn. 6:3-6) and the priority of outreach to unbelievers (Matt. 15:21-28; Mk. 7:3). Second, the miracles were used to reveal conditions of the future messianic kingdom. Jesus' miracles foreshadowed the removal of sickness (Jn. 5:1-18), death (Jn. 11:17-44) and hunger (Matt. 15:32-38). The miracles also point to the joy and prosperity which will characterize God's kingdom (Jn. 2:1-11). Third, the miracles serve to display Jesus' mercy and compassion on suffering humanity (Mk. 1:41, Lk. 7:13; Matt. 14:14, 15:32). Jesus' healing miracles outnumber all the other miracles and demonstrate God's great heart of compassion for humankind (Exod. 34:6).

Jesus' Feeding the Five Thousand
John 6:4-15

Other than Jesus' resurrection, there is one miracle that stands out from the others. The miracle of Jesus' feeding of the five-thousand has a place of prominence in that it is the only one which is recorded in all four Gospels (Matt. 14:15-21; Mk. 6:35-44; Lk. 9:12-17; Jn. 6:4-15). While each of the four gospels records the same event, John's gospel is longer and provides some additional details. John records that the miracle took place as the

Passover was approaching (Jn. 6:4) and reports how the people responded to the miraculous feeding (Jn. 6:15).

Because of the increasing ministry demands, Jesus had invited His apostles to withdraw to a quiet place on the northeast shore of the Sea of Galilee for some rest and spiritual refreshment. He said, "Come away by yourselves to a secluded place and rest for a while (Mk. 6:31). But their time of rest was interrupted by the spiritually needy people of the region who found Jesus with His apostles and sought His help. Seeing them as "sheep without a shepherd," Jesus responded with compassion and began teaching about the Kingdom of God and healing the sick (Mk. 6:34; Lk. 9:11).

Toward evening, the apostles suggested to Jesus that He send the people back to the villages where they could find food and lodging, since they were in such a remote place. But Jesus replied, "They do not need to go away; you give them something to eat" (Matt. 14:16). Phillip recognized the impossibility of feeding such a crowd and said, "Where shall we buy bread for these people to eat?" (Jn. 6:5). Such an expenditure wasn't in the budget and there was no Costco nearby! Andrew, somewhat more optimistic, went out to see what he could gather from the crowd and returned with a little boy's lunch containing five barley loaves and two small fish (Jn. 6:9). This seemed like a joke. What could they do with such meager resources?

Jesus had the apostles right where He wanted them. When serving others, Jesus' disciples need to recognize their own insufficiency and depend totally on Him. Jesus took the little boy's lunch, offered a prayer of thanksgiving for the food and began breaking apart the loaves and the fish. He handed the food to the apostles and they distributed it to the people until "they all ate and were satisfied" (Matt. 14:20). After the meal, Jesus instructed the apostles to pick up the leftovers and they gathered twelve baskets full. Jesus not only provided for the five thousand men and their families, He made sure there was plenty of food for each of the apostles!

After dinner, when Jesus was about to dismiss the crowd to return home, He heard the people begin to say, "Surely this is the Prophet who is to come into the world" (Jn. 6:14). They must have recalled the words of Moses promising that God would raise up "a prophet like me" (Deut. 18:15) whom they must hear and obey. They may have also been influenced by the Jewish expectation that the Messiah would renew the miracle of manna (2 Baruch 29:8, Psa. 132:15, Sibylline Oracle ii.49). Knowing that they were about to "come and make Him king by force" (Jn. 6:15), Jesus immediately dismissed the crowd and went up on a nearby mountain to pray (Matt. 14:23).

Jesus knew that the people's response to His miracle was superficial. The people saw in Jesus someone who could provide for their physical needs and, perhaps, lead them in their struggle against Rome. Imagine their excitement over the prospect of embracing a kingly leader and provider! Yet, this was a superficial offer of kingship. Although they wanted to make Him their king, Jesus understood what they really wanted was a "Burger King."

Jesus' Cleansing the Temple
John 2:13-22

As a faithful Jew, Jesus went to Jerusalem to attend the annual Passover feast which commemorated Israel's deliverance from bondage in Egypt. As required by law, the Passover pilgrims needed a lamb for sacrifice and a Jewish half-shekel for the temple offering. The people living in Jerusalem were quite willing to provide for these needs at highly inflated prices. In fact, the courtyard around the sanctuary had been turned into a market place. John records that in the temple courtyard people "were selling oxen and sheep and doves, and the money changers [were] seated at their tables" (Jn. 2:14). One can imagine the noise, commotion and smells rising from the temple market place. It must have been distracting and disturbing for those who came to the temple to worship.

You may be surprised, as I am, to read of how Jesus reacted to this situation. "And He made a scourge of cords, and drove them all out of the temple, with the sheep and the oxen; and He poured out the coins of the money changers and overturned their tables" (Jn. 2:15). Addressing the startled merchants, Jesus said, "Take these things away; stop making My Father's house a place of business" (Jn. 2:16). This was not a gentle Jesus, merely doing a little cleanup work at the temple. Out of His zeal for God and the sanctity of His temple, Jesus was judging and expelling greedy merchants from what was divinely appointed as a holy place. Jesus' disciples would later recall the words of David which found their ultimate fulfillment in Jesus, "Zeal for Your house will consume Me" (Ps. 69:9; Jn. 2:17).

The Jewish religious leaders, who were in charge of the temple courtyard where the merchants had been selling and changing money, didn't question the legitimacy of Jesus' action. They just questioned Jesus' authority. "What sign do you show us as your authority for doing these things"? (Jn. 2:18). Jesus responded by giving them a riddle. "Destroy this temple, and in three days I will raise it up" (Jn. 2:19). These words really puzzled the Jewish leaders. How could Jesus destroy and raise up the monumental temple sanctuary which had been completely rebuilt by Herod forty-six years earlier? Not even Jesus' disciples understood at the time what Jesus was talking about. The Apostle John points out that it was only after His resurrection that Jesus' disciples remembered His words and understood the riddle as referring to the "temple of His body" (Jn. 2:21). Jesus' words about the destruction and rebuilding of the temple was actually a prophecy of His own death and resurrection!

Jesus' Encounter with Nicodemus
John 3:1-15

Jesus engaged in many conversations about His mission and ministry. One of the most memorable conversations was with a prominent Pharisee named Nicodemus. In addition to being a member of the Sanhedrin (Jn. 7:50), Israel's supreme court, Nicodemus was highly regarded as "the" teacher in Israel (Jn. 3:10). Most importantly, this man was spiritually perceptive. He had witnessed some of the "signs" or miracles which Jesus had done in Jerusalem during the recent Passover and he recognized the significance of Jesus' miracles. He approached Jesus, addressing Him as "Rabbi" (meaning "my master"), a title of respect when addressing a recognized teacher. Nicodemus observed, "We know that You have come from God as a teacher; for no one can do these signs that You do unless God is with him" (Jn. 3:2).

Jesus responded to Nicodemus with startling abruptness. He discerned Nicodemus' spiritual need and his real concern--entrance into God's kingdom. Jesus told Nicodemus very simply, "Truly, truly, I say to you, unless one is born again he cannot see the kingdom of God" (Jn. 3:3).

It was believed by most first century Jews that their ethnic heritage, as descendants of Abraham, Isaac and Jacob, guaranteed their entrance into God's family and heirs of His future kingdom. But Jesus was telling Nicodemus, "That's not enough!" Nicodemus' physical birth ("born of water") made him Jewish. But spiritual rebirth, accomplished by the internal workings of the Holy Spirit, was the singular requirement for enjoying God's kingdom blessings (Jn. 3:5). Jesus emphasized the point by repeating His words, "You must be born again" (Jn. 3:3,7), literally, "born from above." Neither self-effort nor physical descent will guarantee entrance into God's kingdom. There is no other way than spiritual rebirth.

Nicodemus was profoundly puzzled by Jesus' words. He wondered, "How can a man be born when he is old?" To illustrate the mystery of spiritual rebirth, Jesus told Nicodemus that it was like the wind. "The wind blows where it wishes and you hear the sound of it, but do not know where it comes from and where it is going; so is everyone who is born of the Spirit" (Jn. 3:8). The wind is a bit of a mystery. You don't know where it is from or where it is going. Similarly, spiritual rebirth cannot be explained by natural laws. It is the work of God—a work of regeneration.

Still puzzled, Nicodemus queried, "How can these things be?" (Jn. 3:9). Jesus reminded Nicodemus that no one has "ascended to heaven" to bring down a message from God, but He, the messianic "Son of Man," has "descended from heaven" with God's message for humanity (Jn. 3:13). Jesus concluded His conversation with Nicodemus by reminding him of the story of Moses lifting up the serpent in the wilderness (Num. 21:8-9). When the Israelites were dying from bites of poisonous serpents, God instructed Moses to make a bronze image of a serpent and raise it up on a pole. As people raised their eyes up to the serpent on the pole, they were healed and their lives spared from death.

As the bronze serpent was lifted up on the pole in the wilderness, so Jesus "must be lifted up" at His crucifixion. As the Israelites were saved from death by looking upon the raised serpent, so looking with faith on Jesus, the crucified sin-bearer, results in salvation and eternal life (Jn. 3:15).

Jesus' Conversation with the Samaritan
John 4:1-42

When the Israelites were deported from their homeland by the conquering Assyrians in 722 B.C., their land was repopulated with foreigners who brought with them their customs and their gods. They became known as "Samaritans," taking the name of the fallen capital of the Northern Kingdom, Samaria. These foreigners intermarried with Israelites, incorporated the worship of Israel's God along with their pagan ways, and eventually built a temple on Mt. Gerizim to compete with the Jewish temple in Jerusalem. Relations between the Jews and the Samaritans worsened when the Jewish ruler, John Hyrcanus, burned the competing temple in 128 B.C. In Jesus' day, the Samaritans were considered apostate and unclean. To be branded a "Samaritan" would be the greatest of insults (Jn. 8:48). When traveling to Jerusalem from Galilee, Jews with religious scruples crossed the Jordan and went through Perea to avoid contamination from the Samaritans. When a Jewish rabbi was asked by a Samaritan, "Where are you going?" he replied, "I am going to Jerusalem to pray." The Samaritan responded, "Would it not be better for you to pray on this blessed mountain [Mt. Gerizim] rather than on that dunghill in Jerusalem!"

It is with this cultural background in mind that we can better appreciate John's account of Jesus' conversation with a Samaritan woman. In traveling to Jerusalem, Jesus could have avoided the region of Samaria by crossing the

54

Jordan and traveling through Perea, the area to the east, as was the pattern of more scrupulous Jews. But it was necessary for Jesus, "the Light of the world" (Jn. 8:12), to bring His message to the Samaritans as well as the Jews.

It was noon when Jesus was sitting by a well which the great patriarch, Jacob, had dug near ancient Shechem (Jn. 4:5). The disciples had gone to the nearby village of Sychar to buy food. As Jesus, weary from travel, waited by Jacob's well, a lone Samaritan woman approached to draw water. Knowing her spiritual need better than she did, Jesus began a conversation with the simple request, "Give Me a drink" (Jn. 4:7). She replied by expressing her puzzlement in that a Jew would ask her, a Samaritan woman, for a drink. To explain her question for readers unfamiliar with the hostility between Jews and Samaritans, John provides a bit of cultural background, "For Jews have no dealings with Samaritans" (Jn. 4:9). This is an understatement to say the least!

Having gained her attention, Jesus gently guided the conversation into a spiritual discussion. He told the woman that if she knew (1) God's gift of salvation, and (2) that He was the Savior, then she could ask and Jesus would give her "living water" (Jn. 4:10). "Living water," unlike water in a pond or cistern, flows from a spring and is clear, cold and fresh. In this context, Jesus used "living water" as an image of spiritual salvation which He had come to provide for the world (cf. Isa. 55:1, Ezek. 47:1, Rev. 22:1). While water from Jacob's well could relieve thirst temporarily, what Jesus offered could relieve spiritual thirst eternally!

The Samaritan woman showed her interest in what Jesus was speaking about with her words, "Sir, give me this water!" (Jn. 4:15). Jesus wanted to quench her spiritual thirst, but first it was necessary for her to recognize her spiritual need. Jesus probed into her personal life to prompt her repentance. Jesus asked, "Go call your husband and come here (Jn. 4:16). The conversation was becoming a little too personal. Too embarrassed by her own scandalous past, she thought it best to change the subject. Shifting the conversation to the current theological debate, she replied, "Our fathers worshiped in this mountain, and you people say that in Jerusalem is the place where men ought to worship. (Jn. 4:20). After Jesus explained that true worship was the matter of the heart, not geographical locations, she brought up another theological controversy about the identity of the promised Messiah. "I know that Messiah is coming [and] when that One comes, He will declare all things to us" (Jn. 4:25). Jesus must have shocked her with His reply, "I who speak to you am He" (Jn. 4:26).

John concludes his account of Jesus' conversation with the Samaritan woman by reporting that, as a result of her witness in her village, many of the Samaritans came to believe in Jesus (Jn. 4:39). The new believers who had first heard the testimony of the Samaritan woman and then received the witness of Jesus said, "We have heard for ourselves and know that this One is indeed the Savior of the world" (Jn. 4:42). These words capture the essential message of John's gospel. Jesus is the Savior of the Jews, the Samaritans and everyone else in between!

Jesus' Appointment of the Twelve
Mark 3:13-19

Jesus was not going about doing God's kingdom work as a "lone ranger." He knew that ministry is best done in partnership with others who share a commitment to follow and serve God. Shortly after His baptism by John, Jesus began calling people to become His followers and join in His kingdom ministry. The apostle John records the call of the fishermen—Andrew and Peter, Philip and Nathanael (Jn. 1:35-51). Matthew records the call of two brothers, James and John (Matt. 4:21-22). Matthew also recounts his own call. In response to the invitation, Matthew left his tax collection booth at Capernaum and followed Jesus (Matt. 9:9).

Eventually, Jesus selected twelve of His disciples to become "apostles." The word "apostle" refers to "someone sent with a message." This was not a new concept in the Jewish culture. In the first century, the Sanhedrin, the ruling body of Jewish religious leaders, sent out messengers or emissaries (*shlichim*) who would announce and report their judicial decisions. Following this well-stablished protocol, Jesus appointed His messengers who would represent Him, speak with His authority and help proclaim His kingdom message.

Mark records that Jesus selected from His disciples twelve men "so that they could be with Him and that He could send them out to preach" (Mk. 3:14). The twelve would be "with Him," learning from Jesus' teaching and the pattern of His spiritual life. But this special companionship was wrought with purpose. Jesus wanted to prepare these men to preach! Mark 3:14 captures the essential ingredients of discipleship. I define discipleship as "personal companionship in preparation for spiritual leadership." Jesus was spending time with His disciples to prepare them for the ministry they would have following his death and return to heaven.

There is one other factor we shouldn't miss in Jesus' appointment of the twelve apostles. Jesus appointed the twelve as messengers in training for a mission. But He also granted them the *authority* to carry out their mission. In demonstration that their message was proclaimed with divine authority, Jesus gave His apostles power to cast out demons (Mk. 3:15). Their authority over demons is one example of the kinds of miraculous powers given to the apostles to authenticate their ministry and their message.

The twelve apostles are identified by name in Mark 3:16-19 and Luke 6:12-16. They include four fishermen (Peter, Andrew, James and John), Philip (whose name suggests a Greek background), Matthew (the tax collector), Nathaniel (also known as Bartholomew), Thomas (who doubted the resurrection), James the son of Alphaeus (about whom little is known), Thaddaeus (also called Judas), Simon the Zealot (a Judean freedom fighter) and Judas Iscariot (who betrayed Jesus). What a diverse group of individuals! Yet Jesus fashioned them into a team in whom He would invest and prepare to carry His message to the first century world.

Why *twelve* apostles? Why not six? Or perhaps 14? Jesus had many disciples. But He appointed just twelve apostles. It has been suggested that Jesus was making a link with the twelve sons of Jacob who became the heads of the twelve tribes of Israel. Some scholars believe that Jesus was creating a new Israel, a new people of God, distinct from the descendants of Jacob. According to this view, the covenant promises of God to His people Israel (Gen. 12:2-3) would be fulfilled by this new people of God (the church) rather than the ethnic people of Israel.

Instead of seeing discontinuity between the twelve tribes of Israel and the twelve apostles, I think it is better to see a spiritual connection. God was not giving up on Israel and transferring His unconditional promises to a new people. More likely, God was *continuing* His work with the people of Israel through the messianic movement that was inaugurated by John and was being advanced by Jesus. God's work among the people of Israel would continue, but it would continue through the person and work of Jesus and the kingdom message proclaimed by His twelve apostles.

Jesus' Sermon on the Mount
Matthew 5-7

Along with its introductory "Beatitudes," Jesus' Sermon on the Mount is probably His best known discourse. But what is this well-known sermon really about?

It is essential for us to understand the historical setting of this popular message. Great multitudes had been gathering around Jesus as He announced the imminent arrival of God's kingdom and authenticated His message with miracles (Matt. 4:17-23). According to the Hebrew Bible, righteousness was the essential requirement for entrance into God's kingdom (Psa. 24:3-6). Having heard Jesus' message and witnessed His miracles, the people were wondering, "Is the righteousness which we have achieved by observing the Jewish law and traditions sufficient for us to gain entrance into God's kingdom?" Jesus answers that question and provides the theme of His sermon in Matthew 5:20, "For I say to you that unless your righteousness surpasses that of the scribes and Pharisees, you will not enter the kingdom of heaven."

It is important to understand that the Sermon on the Mount is not a message addressed to committed believers who have embraced Jesus and His kingdom offer, but to curious learners who are considering His messianic claims. The addressees are called "disciples" (Matt. 5:1), a Greek word (*mathetes*) which means "learner." The people who heard the Sermon on the Mount were interested in Jesus' teaching, but had yet to commit themselves to Him as Israel's promised Messiah. Some disciples eventually became believers. But John 6:66 records how some of the "learners" who were following Jesus stopped learning and departed from Him.

Throughout this sermon, Jesus is inviting His "learners" to commit themselves to Him as believers. This is evident by the invitation in Matt. 6:33, "But seek first His kingdom and His righteousness, and all these things will be added to you" (see also Matt. 7:5,11,28). The main point of the sermon is that the righteousness that the Jewish people have achieved through their law keeping and good works is insufficient to qualify them for entrance into God's kingdom. In the main body of the of the sermon, Jesus seeks to convict His listeners of their need for the Messiah and the righteousness that comes through faith.

While upholding the Mosaic law (Matt. 5:17-20), Jesus rejected traditional and superficial interpretations of the biblical commandments. Jesus was calling for heart righteousness over against mere hand righteousness. He was calling for inner conformity to the spirit of the law rather than mere outward conformity to the letter of the law. Jesus' emphasis on the true requirements of the law was intended to convict His listeners of their need for Him as the source of true righteousness.

Jesus' Kingdom Ethics
Matthew 7:12, John 13:34-35, Matthew 22:35-40

Did Jesus teach a systematic theology detailing what His followers had to believe? It seems that He was more interested in how they *behaved*. The doctrinal teachings of Christianity would be developed and taught later by men like the apostles Peter, Paul, and John. But Jesus did give us an example to follow (Jn. 13:15, 1 Pet. 2:21) and some ethical principles to live by.

Undoubtedly, the most well known of Jesus' ethical principles is the Golden Rule. Confucius said, "Don't do to others what you don't want done to you." Hillel the Elder, a rabbi who lived a century before Jesus said, "That which is hateful to you, do not do to your fellow. That is the whole Torah. The rest is explanation." But Jesus switched the Golden Rule from the negative to the positive, from reactive to proactive. He said, "Treat people in the same way you want them to treat you, for this is the Law and the Prophets" (Matt. 7:12).

During His last Passover meal with His disciples, Jesus revealed another ethical principle which was especially applicable to His followers. Jesus instituted a new commandment. God instructed the people of Israel, "You shall love your neighbor as yourself" (Lev. 19:18). But Jesus raised the level of love up a notch. He called His disciples to "love one another, even as I have loved you" (Jn. 13: 34). The Greek verb translated "love" is *agapao*) which is a selfless, sacrificial love which looks out for the ultimate good of others. Jesus explained that this *agape* (noun form of *agapao*) love would be the ultimate identifying mark of a follower of Jesus. "By this all men will know that you are My disciples, if you have love for one another" (Jn. 13:35). Jesus gave us a pattern for loving others by His own example as He laid down his life as a sacrifice for humanity's sin. Jesus didn't give us a list of "do's and don'ts." Instead, He showed us how to love one another.

According to Jewish tradition, the Hebrew Bible contains 613 commandments. There are 365 prohibitions and 248 positive commandments. With so many commandments to keep track of, the Jewish people debated with one another what should be the highest priority on the list. One day a Jewish lawyer approached Jesus with a question as to what commandment was highest on his list. "Teacher, which is the great commandment in the Law?" (Matt. 22:36). Jesus answered the lawyer's question by quoting Scripture. Jesus identified the greatest commandment with Deuteronomy 6:5, "You shall love the LORD your God with all your heart, and with all your soul, and with all your mind" (Matt. 22:37). Jesus then went beyond the lawyer's question by identifying the second greatest commandment, "You shall love your neighbor as yourself" (Lev. 19:18; Matt. 22:39). To this instruction Jesus added a comment, "On these two commandments depend the whole Law and the Prophets" (Matt. 22:40). In other words, the biblical revelation in the five books of the Torah and the sixteen Prophets is captured and condensed in the two "great" commandments.

Jesus didn't teach that doing the right thing could *earn* someone a place in God's kingdom. Personal salvation and entrance into God's kingdom comes through faith, not works (Jn. 3:16-18). But He clearly revealed that God would judge and reward His people based on their behavior. God honoring behavior will someday be rewarded (Matt. 6:4). Behavior which reflects unbelief and open rebellion against God's rule will lead to terrible, eternal consequences (Matt. 25:41). Jesus taught that "as every good tree bears good fruit," and every "bad tree bears bad fruit (Matt. 7:17), so the attitude of a person's heart will be evidenced by how they behave. Ethics is not peripheral, but integral to the teaching of Jesus. Mike Beaumont aptly states in *The One-Stop Guide to Jesus,* "For Jesus, *doing* good came out of *being* good" (p. 68).

Jesus' Teaching on Prayer
Matthew 6:9-13; Luke 11:2-4

Fasting, giving alms and prayer were regarded as the three pillars of first century Judaism. Jesus' disciples would have been familiar with the concept of prayer. It was the custom to pray at meals, during synagogue services and at the Jewish festivals. But Jesus' disciples, like many of His followers today, felt that their prayers were inadequate. They wanted to learn how to communicate more effectively with their Creator. One day the disciples asked Jesus, "Lord, teach us to pray" (Lk. 11:1). Jesus responded to His disciples request by teaching them what has traditionally been called "The Lord's Prayer."

The Lord's Prayer is the best known and beloved prayer of Jesus' followers. Most Christians have it memorized. Many churches recite the Lord's prayer regularly as part of their Sunday morning liturgy. I enjoy taking travelers to a church on Jerusalem's Mount of Olives called *Pater Noster* (Latin for "Our Father") where the Lord's prayer appears on the surrounding walls in 167 different languages! According to tradition, the church was built over a cave venerated as the location where Jesus taught his disciples the prayer. I always conclude our visit at the site by inviting our group to say the Lord's Prayer together.

Matthew sets the Lord's Prayer in the context of His Sermon on the Mount. He begins by providing corrections on the traditional Jewish practice of prayer. Some were hypocrites who used public prayer as a means of gaining attention and recognition from others. Jesus advised His disciples to pray in private with the assurance that "your Father who sees what is done in secret will reward you" (Matt. 6:6). Jesus also advised against using meaningless repetition in prayer, pointing out that it was not the form or length of a prayer that made it effective since "your Father knows what you need before you ask" (Matt. 6:8).

The prayer Jesus taught his disciples was not something to be pronounced mindlessly by rote memory. This is evident by the differences or variation between the two "Lord's Prayers" in Matthew 6 and Luke 11. What Jesus was teaching His disciples was a *pattern* for prayer. The first part of the Lord's Prayer focuses on God's interests—His name (reputation), His kingdom, and His will (Matt. 6:9-10). The second part of the prayer addresses our personal needs—our daily food, our need for forgiveness, and our temptations to sin (Matt. 6:11-13).

In addition to Jesus' major teaching on prayer in Matthew 6:9-13 and Luke 11:2-4, Jesus provided His disciples with other important principles of prayer. First, Jesus taught that prayer should be an expression of faith. "And all things you ask in prayer, believing, you will receive" (Matt. 21:22). Second, He taught that prayer should be persistent. In the parable of the persistent widow, Jesus revealed that we should pray and not give up, even when it appears that the answer is not forthcoming, just as the widow eventually got what she needed because she persisted in petitioning the judge (Luke 18:1-8). Finally, Jesus taught that his followers should appeal to their heavenly Father in the name of Jesus, God's son (Jn. 14:13-14; 16:23-24). To appeal to the Father in the name of Jesus is to ask the Father to answer based on the merits and influence of His Son. It is something like signing Jesus' name to our prayers. When we pray to the Father in the name of Jesus, we can be confident that God will answer our prayer according to His perfect will.

Jesus' Rejection by Israel
Matthew 12:22-32

Matthew witnessed and recorded many important events in the life of Jesus. But there was one key turning point that is frequently missed when reading the gospel. We usually think of Israel's rejection of Jesus as taking place at His trial and crucifixion, but Jesus' rejection by the leaders of Israel took place much earlier. Jesus' rejection by the leaders ultimately led to His rejection by the Jewish people.

Matthew tells of how Jesus did a great miracle. He liberated a man who was being tormented by a demon (Matt. 12:22). The people were amazed! The miracle pointed to the fact that Jesus was the promised Messiah who had come to "set the captives free" (Isa. 61:1-2a).

But the Jewish religious leaders didn't buy it. The Pharisees couldn't deny the fact that a great miracle had taken place. So they said that Jesus had "cast out demons only by Beelzebul, the ruler of the demons" (Matt. 12:24). They were saying that Jesus had done the miracle by Satan's power! They were telling the people of Israel that Jesus' credentials are of hell, not heaven!"

If this view prevailed, Jesus would be rejected and His kingdom rule would have to be postponed. Jesus responded by showing that the arguments of the Jewish leaders were absurd, inconsistent and illogical. It was *absurd* to think that Satan would cast out Satan (Matt. 12:25-26). How could such a divided kingdom survive? It was *inconsistent* to say that Jesus cast out demons by Satan's power while reputed Jewish exorcists did the same thing by God's power (Matt. 12:27). Finally, it was *illogical* to suggest that He was merely human. After all, Jesus had entered Satan's domain and delivered one of his captives (Matt. 12:29). Jesus, by the power of the Holy Spirit (Matt. 12:28), had released Satan's captive, in demonstration of God's kingdom reign and rule!

Many readers of Matthew's gospel have been troubled by the words of verse 31, "Therefore I say to you, any sin and blasphemy shall be forgiven people, but blasphemy against the Spirit shall not be forgiven." Does this mean that people living in the 21st century can commit a sin that God won't forgive? The key to solving this interpretive problem is to understand the immediate, historical context. Matthew is describing a first century situation where Jesus was on earth doing miracles by the power of the Holy Spirit with the expectation that the Jewish nation would respond and accept Him as their Messiah. The circumstances of this unusual sin cannot be reproduced today. Since the historical situation cannot be reproduced, the sin cannot be repeated.

Careful study of this unique sin in its historical context has led me to conclude that no sin committed in the 21st century can be regarded as unforgivable. Even the sin of unbelief can be forgiven through faith and repentance (Acts 3:19; 4:12; 16:31).

Jesus was simply saying to the first century Jewish leaders that in rejecting the evidence of His miracles, they have committed a sin that was so contrary and damaging to God's purposes for Israel that it would never be forgiven. In their desperate attempt to turn the people away from following Jesus, they had declared that His miracles were the works of Satan rather than God. Their explanation set the nation of Israel on the course of rejecting Jesus, Israel's promised Messiah.

Whatever might be your interpretation of the "unpardonable sin," understand that this event was a *key turning point* in the life of Christ. From this point on, things would be different. The Jewish leadership had rejected Jesus' messianic credentials. There would be no further signs for the nation of Israel except one—the "sign of Jonah" (Matt. 13:38-41), the resurrection of Jesus. From this point on in His life and ministry, Jesus would be preparing His disciples for His impending rejection and execution.

Jesus' Teaching the Kingdom Parables
Matthew 13

With Jesus' rejection by the Jewish religious leaders, the disciples must have realized that a trajectory had been set which would lead to Jesus' rejection by the people of Israel. It was in light of this situation that they had some important questions about the promised kingdom. Jesus' disciples wondered: "With the rejection of Jesus by Israel's leaders, what is going to happen to God's kingdom program? Has the kingdom Jesus announced been cancelled? How will God continue His work on earth until His kingdom purposes are accomplished?"

Jesus began to answer these questions by teaching His disciples through the parables (Matt. 13:1-52). The parables serve to reveal truth to receptive disciples and conceal truth from those who are rejecting Jesus (Matt. 13:10-17). The parables disclose some new truths about God's kingdom program as it develops during the period of Messiah's rejection by Israel. The parables teach how God's kingdom will grow spiritually during the period between His rejection and His future acceptance by Israel.

The parables reveal that God's kingdom program has not been cancelled by Israel's rejection of King Jesus. Like seed sown in a field, there would be a proclamation of kingdom news in the present age (Matt. 13:3-9). Like seed falling on different terrain, there would be varying responses to the kingdom message (Matt. 13:18-23). Like the mustard seed, the kingdom will start small and grow large (Matt. 13:31-32). Like leaven in dough, the kingdom will grow by an internal dynamic (Matt. 13:33). Like a great treasure, the kingdom is worth pursuing and sacrificing for (Matt. 13:44-46). Like fishermen who keep the good fish and toss away the bad, so God will be the judge of those seeking entrance into the kingdom (Matt. 13:47-50).

Jesus' Promise to Build the Church
Matthew 16:13-20

What do most people think of when they hear the word "church"? Although you may be an exception, most people think of a church *building*. In fact, the word "church" is derived from the Old English *kirche* meaning "a building for Christian worship." But the Greek word translated "church" (*ekklesia*) is not a place, but a people—a congregation. Matthew 16 records Jesus' promise to build his church—a messianic congregation or community of Jesus' followers.

This promise was made when Jesus and His disciples were visiting the district of Caesarea Philippi at the foot of 9,200-foot Mount Hermon. This is a lovely setting featuring the headwaters of the Banias stream that gushes forth from springs to become one of the three sources of the Jordan River. But it was also a place of pagan worship. Caesarea was the sanctuary of the nature god Pan, who was half man and half goat. Pan was associated with eroticism and the natural world of hills, woods, flocks and herds. The city of Caesarea Philippi was rebuilt by King Herod's son, Philip and named after Caesar Augustus.

It was here, in the vicinity of a false worship center, that Jesus asked His disciples for a report on the interpretation of His person by the people of Israel. "Who do people say that the Son of Man is?" (Matt. 16:13). Many of the first century Jews recognized Jesus as some sort of messenger from God (Matt. 16:14). But Jesus wanted to know the opinion of his disciples. Peter answered for the twelve, "You are the Messiah, the Son of the living God" (Matt. 16:16). Peter gets and "A" for the day with his correct answer. Jesus is Israel's promised Messiah and God's divine Son. After pronouncing a blessing on Peter for his good answer, Jesus announced the formation of a messianic community.

Jesus makes a play on words in verse 18 which can be best appreciated with some knowledge of the Greek words. Peter's (*Petros*) name means "a small, movable rock or pebble." Jesus announced that His messianic congregation would be built on a *petra*, an immovable rock formation. Jesus is telling Peter and the disciples that He was going to build the church on something much stronger and immovable than Peter, a mere pebble. So what *is* the *petra*? What *was* the rock-solid foundation of the messianic congregation Jesus was gathering and building? Some say that Jesus Himself is the rock. This view fits well with other scripture (1 Cor. 10:4; Eph. 2:22; 1 Pet. 2:6-8), but I think there is a better view. I suggest that the *truth* of Peter's confession—that Jesus is Israel's Messiah, the Son of God—is the rock-solid foundation of the church. The congregation of God's people in Christ rests on no more fundamental truth that this!

Jesus went on to promise that while the congregation of His people may come under attack by Satan, the enemy will not prevail (Matt. 16:18). Jesus' death will not prevent the congregation's establishment. And Satan's schemes will not prevail against it.

It should not surprise us to see how the congregation of Jesus' followers has grown since the first century. Nor should it surprise us to witness the persecution of the congregation of God's people today! Yet, the Spirit-empowered church that Jesus promised to build keeps on growing! By the end of the first century, there were Christians in every key city in the Roman empire. Now in the 21st century we find congregations of Jesus' followers in every country around the world.

Jesus' Transfiguration
Matthew 17:1-13

As the end of His life on earth drew near, Jesus began preparing His disciples for His death (16:21). But the disciples feared that Jesus' death would prevent the establishment of the promised kingdom (16:22). How could Jesus, Israel's Messiah, die and yet claim David's throne in the messianic kingdom? The transfiguration of Jesus was intended to deal with this issue.

Jesus' transfiguration took place on a "high mountain" (Matt. 17:1). The gospel account does not identify on which mountain in Israel the event took place. Mount

Tabor has been the traditional location of the transfiguration. Although the summit features a lovely church and provides a sweeping view of the Jezreel Valley, the 1800-foot elevation hardly qualifies as a "high mountain." Since Jesus had recently been with His disciples in the district of Caesarea Philippi (Matt. 16:13), the early readers of Matthew's gospel would expect to find the "high mountain" in this vicinity. It may well have been on 9200-foot Mount Hermon, just north of Caesarea Philippi, that Jesus was "changed from the inside out" (*metamorphoo*) before Peter, James and John.

In this amazing miracle, Jesus' face "shone like the sun, and His garments became white as light" (Matt. 17:2). It seems as though the deity of Jesus radiated out through His human flesh! Peter, James and John were there to witness the event, and two of these men mention it in their later writings (2 Pet. 1:16-18; Jn. 1:14).

Two visitors from Israel's past appeared with Jesus at His transfiguration—Moses (the great lawgiver) and Elijah (the great prophet). Moses had died and Elijah had been taken to heaven in a whirlwind. The presence of these bygone visitors demonstrate that departure from this world would not hinder the establishment of Jesus' kingdom. Death was not the end for Moses and Elijah. And so Jesus' death would not mean an end to Israel's kingdom hope!

Jesus' transfiguration was culminated with God speaking once again from heaven. He repeated the words spoken at Jesus' baptism, "This is my beloved Son in whom I am well pleased" (Matt. 3:17). But then He added, "Listen to Him!" (Matt. 17:5). In other words, "Pay attention to His teaching." This instruction is an echo from

Deuteronomy 18:15, where Moses predicted the coming of "a prophet like me" to whom the people of Israel must "listen." Some Galileans had earlier suggested that Jesus was the promised prophet (Jn. 6:14).

Jesus' Royal Entry into Jerusalem
Matthew 21:1-11

While this event is often referred to as Jesus' "Triumphal Entry," I suggest that this designation applies better to His Second Coming. His first coming resulted in Jesus' rejection and crucifixion. Not exactly a "triumph." But it was certainly a "royal entry" as Israel's promised king. The royal entry of Jesus into Jerusalem was the official presentation of the Jesus to the nation of Israel as their promised Messiah. He came in the prescribed way (Zech. 9:9) and on the prophesied day (Lk. 19:42). The events that followed Jesus' royal entry into Jerusalem constitute the official response of the nation to the official presentation of Israel's Messiah.

According to his careful research into the chronology of events in the life of Christ, Harold Hoehner has argued that the royal entry took place on Monday, rather than Sunday (*Chronological Aspects of the Life of Christ,* pp. 90-94). This corresponds with the fact that Monday was the 10th of Nisan—the very day that the Passover lamb was selected for sacrifice (Exod. 12:3). It was on this day that Jesus was presented as Israel's true Passover Lamb.

Jesus came into Jerusalem riding on a donkey—a royal mount—in fulfillment of the prophecy of Zechariah

9:9. As Jesus approached the city, the people showed Him honor by spreading their garments on the road before Him (Mk. 11:8) and waving palm branches (Jn. 12:13). The crowd following Jesus to Jerusalem began shouting, "Hosanna!" This Hebrew word means "Save us now!" The Jewish people were appealing for Jesus to take up arms against Rome and save them from their enemies. They were rejoicing because they believed their Messiah had come and they were appealing for Jesus to take His rightful throne and "save" them from Roman rule and oppression.

But the crowd was flippant and was easily convinced by the Jewish religious leaders that Jesus was a false messiah. The Jewish leadership had managed to convince the people that Jesus had done His miracles by Satan's power rather than by the power of the Holy Spirit (Matt. 12:22-32). Later that week, under the influence of their religious leaders, the same people who had shouted "Hosanna," would cry out for Jesus' crucifixion.

Jesus' Predictions about Israel's Future
Matthew 24-25

Even though the nation of Israel had rejected their Messiah, God wasn't through with them. The psalmist reminds us, "The Lord will not abandon His people, nor will He forsake His inheritance" (Psa. 94:14). Although Jerusalem would be judged and destroyed in A.D. 70 by the Romans (Matt. 23:38), Jesus anticipates a day when

His people will repent and embrace Him at His Second Coming (Zech. 12:10-13:1; Rom. 11:26).

Scholars debate whether the prophecies in Jesus' Olivet Discourse were fulfilled in the past when the Romans destroyed Jerusalem (A.D. 70) or are being fulfilled now during the present age. I believe that the events described by Jesus in the message given to His disciples on the Mount of Olives will be filled in the future. This interpretation reflects a consistently literal understanding of Scripture, recognizing that what Jesus predicted has not yet been literally fulfilled.

As Jesus ascended the Mount of Olives on His way back to Bethany, His disciples pointed out the lovely buildings on the temple platform. Jesus responded by announcing that the beautiful temple buildings would one day be totally destroyed. He said, "Not one stone will be left upon another, which will not be torn down (Matt. 24:2). No doubt disturbed by these words, Jesus' disciples responded with two questions: (1) When will the temple be destroyed? (2) What will be the sign of Messiah's coming and the end of the age? The answer to the first question is found in Luke 21:20-24 where Jesus describes the coming destruction of Jerusalem by the Romans in A.D. 70. The second question is about eschatology—the events of the last days. Zechariah 14:1-8 reveals that the end of the present age coincides with the coming of Israel's messiah. Matthew's record of Jesus' Mount of Olives message answers the second question. In Matthew's record of the Olivet Discourse, Jesus presents the signs of Messiah's coming, which would mark the end of the present age.

While there is a great deal of debate about the details of this important prophecy, I believe there are three main points that Jesus is highlighting in this message about the Messiah's coming and the end of the age. *First,* it will be longer than you expect, so be wise and discerning (Matt. 24:4-5). *Second*, it will be harder than you expect, so be prepared and persistent (24:9-14). *Third*, it will be better than you expect, so be encouraged and hopeful (24:27-31).

There has been a great deal of speculation over the centuries since Jesus spoke these words as to the time when these prophecies will be fulfilled. Some preachers have been so daring (and foolish) to predict the actual time of Jesus' return! But Jesus points out that no one knows the day or the hour of His return. Jesus said, "But of that day and hour no one knows, not even the angels of heaven, nor the Son, but the Father alone" (Matt. 24:36). Anyone who believes they can predict the date of Jesus' return clearly hasn't paid attention to these words!

Since no one knows when the prophesied events will occur, Jesus uses parables to highlight the need to be alert, watchful and prepared (Matt. 24:32-51). The time of Jesus' return is likened to the days of Noah when people were going about their everyday tasks and failing to heed the warnings. As a result, the flood came and swept them away! In light of Jesus' prophecies about the future, His disciples must take heed and be prepared. Jesus said,

"You also must be ready; for the Son of Man is coming at an hour when you do not think He will" (Matt. 25:44).

Jesus' Last Passover
John 13-16

On the night before His trial and execution, Jesus shared a Passover meal with His twelve apostles. The meal is remembered in church tradition as Jesus' last supper. It might better be remembered as his last Passover. It was Thursday, Nisan 14 of the year A.D.33 when Jesus gathered with His twelve apostles in the upper room of a house in Jerusalem, probably the house of Mary, mother of John Mark (Acts 1:13; 12:12).

The first thing of significance was that the Last Supper was a Passover meal which followed the traditional Jewish Passover ritual. Jesus would have observed Passover with his own family and with His disciples on other occasions. He would have been familiar with each of the traditional foods on the Passover plate, ritual washings, prayers and songs which were part of a Jewish Passover.

Although Jesus followed the order of service of the traditional Jewish Passover, He modified the service to teach an important lesson. The Passover Seder included a ritual of hand washing. But when the disciples expected Jesus to lead in the ritual of passing a bowl for the disciples to dip their fingers, Jesus arose from the supper, girded himself with a towel, and began washing the disciples' feet (Jn. 13:2-5). Foot washing was customarily

78

a servant's job, and Jesus was taking upon Himself the role of a servant to wash the disciple's feet. Of course Peter protested this reversal of roles and told Jesus, "Never shall you wash my feet" (Jn. 13:8). But Jesus told Peter that to refuse His service was tantamount to rejecting His person and work! Peter relented and Jesus finished the procedure, washing and drying twelve pairs of feet.

When He had finished the task, Jesus provided an explanation. "You call Me Teacher and Lord, and you are right, for so I am. If then, the Lord and the Teacher, washed your feet, you also ought to wash one another's feet. For I gave you an example that you also should do as I did to you" (Jn. 13:13-16). By His example, Jesus had taught the twelve apostles a life-defining principle. Ministry is essentially service--humble service to others. Whatever role a disciple may assume in the community of Jesus' followers, the ultimate, bottom line in ministry is serving others out of love and commitment for Jesus.

It was customary during the Passover meal for there to be some teaching. Jesus took this last opportunity after the Passover meal to instruct His disciples on a number of important topics. The sign of circumcision marked and identified the people of Israel. Jesus introduced His disciples to a new sign that would mark them as His followers. It was the sign of *love* for one another. "By this all men will know that you are My disciples if you have love for one another" (Jn. 13:35). Jesus also taught His disciples about heaven, the place He was going away to prepare for them (Jn. 14:2-3). One of the special teachings Jesus gave His disciples during His upper room discourse was on the subject of prayer. He instructed His followers to pray to the Father in the name of Jesus, assuring them that prayers offered in Jesus' name would assuredly receive the Father's answer (Jn. 14:12-14). Jesus also taught His disciples that although He was going away, He would not leave them alone. The Holy Spirit would be their ever present helper, empowering, encouraging and teaching them (Jn. 14:26; 15:26-27; 16:12-14). Jesus warned His disciples that they were going to face the unbelieving world's hatred and hostility (Jn. 15:18-25), to such a degree that it may result in their deaths (Jn. 16:1-4). Jesus told His disciples that the days ahead weren't going to be easy. There would be great sorrow over His death, but that would be replaced by joy at His resurrection (Jn. 16:20-22). While they would go through testing and tribulation, they could have peace and victory in Him (Jn. 16:33).

Before leaving the upper room for the Garden of Gethsemane, where He would be betrayed by Judas and arrested by the Roman soldiers, Jesus gave the disciples a memorial by which he wanted to be remembered. What is usually referred to as "the Lord's Supper" is really a part of the Passover Supper which Jesus adapted as a memorial to His own person and work. Among the traditional items featured in the Passover meal were unleavened bread (*matzah*) and cups of wine. The unleavened bread recalled the fact that the Israelites left Egypt in such a hurry that they didn't have time to let the bread rise (Exod. 12:15,39). The wine recalled the blood of the Passover lamb that was placed on the doorposts of the Israelite houses. The application of the blood reflected their faith in God's provision and redeemed the first born sons from the death plague (Exod. 12:7,13).

Jesus took these two Passover symbols and enhanced their significance (Matt. 26:26-28). The unleavened bread would now become a reminder of Jesus, "the Bread of Life" (Jn. 6:35). The wine would now become a reminder of Jesus, "the Lamb of God who takes away the sin of the world" (Jn. 1:29). Paul explains that eating the unleavened bread and drinking from the cup serves as a reminder of Jesus' person and work (1 Cor. 11:24-25). But eating the *matzah* and drinking from the Passover cup is more than a reminder. Paul adds that eating the Passover bread and drinking from the Passover cup is a corporate *proclamation* of the ultimate sacrifice for sins which Jesus accomplished on the cross at Golgotha (1 Cor. 11:26). Everyone who participates in communion is, in effect, shouting to the world the good news of God's provision of salvation through Savior Jesus.

Jesus' Arrest and Trial
Matthew 26:57-27:26

After his arrest in the Garden of Gethsemane, Jesus was tried first by the Jewish authorities and then by the Romans. The two-part trial was necessitated because the Jewish authorities, who wanted Jesus executed, didn't have the legal authority to put Him to death. The power of capital punishment was the ultimate sign of the tightly held Roman civil authority in the providence of Judea.

Jesus religious trial began in the court of Annas, the Jewish high priest from A.D. 6 to A.D. 15, when He was deposed by the Romans. Since the high priest was supposed to hold his office for life (Num. 35:25, 28), Annas retained his title and authority even after his removal from office by the Romans. After the preliminary examination of Jesus, Annas gave his consent to proceed with the Sanhedrin examination (John 18:12-24).

The next phase of Jesus religious trial was in the court of Caiaphas, the son-in-law of Annas who served as high priest and president of the Sanhedrin from A.D. 18 to A.D. 36 (Mk. 14:53-65). This was a secret and illegal examination by the Sanhedrin since it took place at night and in the house of Caiaphas rather than the official meeting place in the temple court. This illegal procedure resulted in an accusation of blasphemy against Jesus (Mk. 14:64).

In the early morning hours of April 3, A.D. 33, the Sanhedrin met again to give their night verdict some semblance of legitimacy (Mk. 15:1). Jesus was then delivered up to the Roman authorities because the Judeans, who wanted Jesus put to death, were not permitted to execute capital punishment (Jn. 18:31).

The Roman trial of Jesus began in the court of Pontius Pilate. Following the expulsion of Herod's son Archelaus in A.D. 6, Judea became a Roman Imperial Province governed by a prefect. Pontus Pilate served as prefect from A.D. 26 to A.D. 36. He normally lived in

Caesarea, but stayed in Jerusalem during Jewish festivals so he would be available to command the Roman troops and to keep order in case of a disturbance. Pilate was staying in the Praetorium (Jn. 18:28), probably Antonia Fortress, when the Jewish religious leaders brought Jesus to him with several damning accusations. They charged, "We found this man misleading our nation and forbidding to pay taxes to Caesar, and saying that He Himself is Messiah, a King" (Lk. 23:2). Pilate examined Jesus, but found no fault in Him (Lk. 23:4).

Although Pilate found Jesus innocent, he referred the case to Herod Antipas (B.C. 4 to A.D. 39), Tetrarch of Galilee and Perea, who was visiting Jerusalem at the time (Lk. 23:6-12). Pilate no doubt wanted to free himself from an awkward case and also sought to improve his relationship with Antipas which had been strained by his massacre of a group of Galileans visiting Jerusalem (Lk. 13:1). Antipas had long desired to see Jesus and perhaps witness some miracle (Lk. 23:8). This diplomatic courtesy resulted in a reconciliation between Pilate and Antipas (Lk. 23:12), but didn't actually advance the legal proceedings of the trial.

After Jesus' appearance in the court of Antipas, the case was returned to Pilate (Mk 15:6-15). The Roman prefect recognized Christ's innocence and attempted to secure His acquittal and release. But Jerusalem's religious leaders persuaded the crowd to demand Jesus' crucifixion. We learn from historical sources that Pilate was very anti-Semitic and hated the Jews. Until A.D. 32 his ruthless policies had been hidden from the Roman emperor by Sejanus, the head of the Praetorian Guard under Tiberius. But in A.D. 32, Sejanus was caught in a plot to usurp the throne of Tiberius. He was brought before the Roman senate, charged and executed. The execution of Sejanus left Pilate without his protector in Rome. With his future political career in jeopardy, Pilate was anxious to avoid trouble in Judea which might be reported to Emperor Tiberius (Jn. 19:12-16). When the people cried out, "If you release this man, you are no friend of Caesar" (Jn. 19:12). Pilate recognized the path of political expediency and yielded to the demands of the crowd (Jn. 19:12-16). Better to let an innocent Galilean die than to jeopardize his own political career! The trial of Jesus was over by about 6:00 A.M. (Jn. 19:14). The verdict was in. Jesus was condemned to death. After being brutally scourged, Jesus was handed over to a contingent of Roman soldiers to be crucified (Matt. 27:26).

Jesus' Crucifixion
Matthew 27:26

Since the time of Jesus, the cross has been a symbol of Christianity. There are crosses in churches, on jewelry, on walls in homes and on grave markers. The cross reminds us of the fact that Jesus died on a cross. The gospel accounts of Jesus' death report that He was crucified. Literary sources indicate that tens of thousands of people were crucified in the Roman Empire. Since most of the first century readers had witnessed the horrors of crucifixion, the gospel writers felt no need to report the graphic details.

Many people assume that crucifixion was a Roman invention. In fact, the Assyrians, Phoenicians, Persians and Greeks all practiced crucifixion. While the traditional method of execution among Jews was stoning (Deut. 21:22-23), Josephus reports that the Hasmonean ruler, Alexander Jannaeus, once crucified 800 Jews on a single day! The Romans adopted crucifixion as the official punishment for non-Romans. During the revolt of Spartacus in 71 B.C., the Roman army lined the road leading to Rome with the crosses of 6,000 crucified rebels. During Titus' siege of Jerusalem in A.D. 70, Roman troops crucified as many as 500 Jews a day for several months.

In the provinces of the Roman Empire, Roman governors alone had the authority to impose the death penalty. When a local, provincial court prescribed the death penalty, authorization from the Roman governor was required in order to carry out the sentence. Once a defendant was found guilty and condemned to be crucified, the execution was supervised by a Roman official known as the *Carnifix Serarum* (literally a "flesh nailer"). Based on Scripture and other literary resources, we can reconstruct the steps that would have been taken in crucifying Jesus.

(1) Jesus was taken from the tribunal hall, stripped, bound to a column and scourged (Matt. 27:26). The scourging was done with either a stick or a *flagellum*, an instrument with a short handle to which several thick

thongs were attached. On the ends of the leather thongs were lead or bone tips. Josephus describes a man whose ribs were laid bare by scourging.

(2) Following the scourging, the horizontal crossbeam of the cross was placed upon Jesus' shoulders. When Jesus stumbled under the weight of the crossbeam, Simon of Cyrene was compelled by the soldiers to help Jesus carry His cross (Matt. 27:32) to the crucifixion site outside Jerusalem's walls.

(3) A soldier at the head of the procession carried the *titulus*, an inscription written on wood, which stated the defendant's name and the crime for which he had been condemned. Later the *titulus* was attached to the victim's cross. The *titulus* on Jesus' cross read, "This is Jesus, the King of the Jews" (Matt. 27:37).

(4) The procession went from Pilate's Praetorium to the place of execution outside Jerusalem's wall called Golgotha (Matt. 27:33) meaning, "Place of a Skull." There a vertical stake was fixed into the ground. Jesus was then raised up on the upright post and His arms fastened to the cross beam. The 1968 discovery of the heel bones of a young, crucified Jew in a Jerusalem tomb has shed light on our understanding of the position of the victim on his cross. The victim's heels had been pinned together by a 7½-inch nail. The nail went through the right heel bone and then the left. Thus, the legs were together, not apart on the cross. The arm bones of the victim revealed a small scratch on one bone just above the wrist. This scratch was made by the nail gliding across the bone. Paintings of Christ usually show nails piercing His hands,

but the weight of the slumping body would have torn the nails out of the palms in a short time unless they were also bound to the crossbeam. While John 20:25 does mention Christ's "hands," the word can also refer to "arms." The discovery of the bones of the crucified man has enabled experts to reconstruct Jesus' position on the cross. His arms were nailed above the wrists to the crossbeam. His legs were bent and twisted to one side, with His feet being attached to the upright post by a nail driven through His ankle bones. It was customary for victims to be crucified naked, adding shame and humiliation to the suffering as victims lost control of their bodily functions.

(5) Without any physical support, a victim hanging on a cross would die from muscular spasms and asphyxiation in a period of two to three hours. In order to prolong the agony, the Romans devised two instruments which would extend the ordeal of the victim. First, a small seat (*sedile*) was attached to the front of the cross. This device provided support for the victim's body and explains the phrase used by the Romans, "to sit on the cross."   A second device was a foot support (*suppedaneum*). The seat and foot support could enable victims of crucifixion to be kept alive on the cross for several days. Josephus refers to three crucified Jews who survived on crosses for three days.

(6) Normally the Romans left the crucified person undisturbed to die slowly of physical exhaustion, thirst, and asphyxiation. However, Jewish law required burial on the day of execution (Deut. 21:22-23). Therefore, in Judea

the execution squad would break the legs of the crucified person in order to hasten his death and thus permit burial before nightfall. The purpose of breaking the legs was not to increase the pain, but to prevent the victim from using his legs to raise his body and inflate his oxygen starved lungs with air. Breaking the legs would quickly lead to death by asphyxiation. John reports that, like Israel's Passover lamb (Exod. 12:46), Jesus' legs were not broken since he died before the onset of Sabbath (Jn. 19:31-33). But to confirm that He was dead, one of the Roman soldiers thrust his spear into Jesus' side, a wound which released blood and water (Jn. 19:34).

Jesus' Death for Sin
Matthew 27:45-54

While Jesus suffered the agony and humiliation of crucifixion, He did not die as a *result* of crucifixion. John reports that Jesus said, "It is finished," and then "bowed His head and gave up His spirit" (Jn. 19:30). No one took Jesus' life from Him. Rather, He freely and voluntarily gave up His life as a sacrifice for the sins of lost humanity.

The death of Jesus was the culmination of God's great plan to deal once and for all with the sins of fallen humanity. All the sacrifices of Israel's past found their ultimate fulfillment in what Jesus accomplished for all people on the cross.

In Matthew 27:46 we read of the most significant moment in redemptive history when Jesus cried out, "My God, My God, why have You forsaken Me?" Like David, who first spoke these words (Psa. 22:1), Jesus had arrived at a very spiritually dark moment. This was the moment when Jesus bore the sins of humanity. Paul explains that when Jesus bore our sins--past, present, and future--He "became sin for us" (2 Cor. 5:21). At that moment, the intimate fellowship which Jesus had enjoyed from eternity past with the Father was broken. To pay the full penalty of our sin and provide salvation, Jesus had to endure spiritual as well as physical death.

In the ultimate moment of His agony, Jesus reached out to His Heavenly Father; and instead of finding God's comforting presence, He felt deserted and forsaken. The wrath of God the Father was being poured out on the sin being shouldered by His Son. In His agony, Jesus felt forsaken by God! This is too great to comprehend or explain. We simply believe it and thank God for His ultimate sacrifice and what it accomplished.

Jesus laid down His life out of love and obedience as a voluntary sacrifice. He took our place on the cross and received the judgment which we deserved for our sins. On the cross, Jesus offered Himself as the perfect Passover Lamb for the sins of the world, satisfying fully God's wrath on sinners. What an amazing and wonderful gift of grace!

Jesus' Burial in a Borrowed Tomb
Matthew 27:57-66

If we believe that Jesus died and rose again, how important is it to know that He was buried? The Apostle Paul seems to think that it was pretty important because he includes it in his description of the essential points of the gospel. Paul wrote to the Corinthians saying, "For I delivered to you as of first importance what I also received, that Jesus died for our sins according to the Scriptures, and that He was buried, ..." (1 Cor. 15:3-4). The burial of Jesus is important because it authenticates His death. Some people say that Jesus didn't actually die. They suggest that Jesus survived the crucifixion and was just hidden away by His apostles. But you don't *bury* someone who is *alive*. The gospel record reveals that Jesus actually *died,* because He was *buried*.

Joseph of Arimathea was a wealthy member of the Sanhedrin (Lk. 23:51) who had not consented to the unjust verdict that resulted in Jesus' crucifixion. He had become a disciple of Jesus, but had kept it a secret (Jn. 19:38). After the death of Jesus, Joseph stepped forward to claim the body of Jesus and provide Him with a proper burial. With the help of Nicodemus (Jn. 19:34), Jesus' body was removed from the cross, wrapped with strips of linen intermingled with spices and placed in Joseph's newly excavated, rock-cut tomb (Matt. 27:59-60; Jn. 19:40-41). Jesus' burial in the borrowed tomb of a rich man fulfilled the prediction by Isaiah the prophet that the Messiah would be "with a rich man in his death" (Isa. 53:9).

Luke and John both point out the fact that it was a tomb "in which no one had ever been laid" (Lk. 23:53; Jn. 19:41). This reflects the Jewish concern for purity. According to Jewish law, contact with a corpse was regarded as ceremonially defiling (Num. 6:6). But since Jesus was buried in a new tomb, it had not been contaminated with the uncleanness of death. A large stone was rolled in front of the tomb to close the entrance (Matt. 27:60).

The day after Jesus' crucifixion, the religious leaders remembered something that the disciples had apparently forgotten. They went to Pilate and said, "Sir, we remember that when He was still alive that deceiver said, 'After three days I am to rise again.' Therefore, give orders for the grave to be made secure until the third day, otherwise His disciples may come and steal Him away," reporting that Jesus had been resurrected (Matt. 27:63-64). This concern shows the importance of the resurrection. The resurrection of Jesus would confirm His messianic claims.

Pilate consented to have the tomb secured and sealed. Several Roman soldiers were sent to guard the tomb and the seal of Rome was placed on the rolling stone (Matt. 27:65-66). Sealed by the highest authority in the Roman world, no one would have dared, or been able, to tamper with Jesus' tomb.

Jesus' Resurrection Before Witnesses
Matthew 28:1-10

The death of Jesus on the cross is not the end of the story! Early in His ministry, Jesus had announced that there would be one last sign to the nation of Israel that would serve to authenticate His messianic claims. Jesus called this "the sign of Jonah" (Matt. 12:39; 16:4). As Jonah had been three days in the belly of the fish, so

Jesus would be in the grave. And, as Jonah was delivered from the fish, so Jesus was resurrected from His grave.

The resurrection of Jesus is the final authentication that He was who He claimed to be—the Son of God and the promised Messiah of Old Testament prophecy. When visitors arrived at the tomb early Sunday morning, the angel announced, "He is not here, for He has risen, just as He said" (Matt. 28:6).

Later that morning, Jesus appeared to Mary; then He appeared to Peter. That evening Jesus appeared to the two disciples on the road to Emmaus; and later to the ten disciples in the Upper Room. Paul records that Jesus appeared to more than five hundred of His followers at one time (1 Cor. 15:6). The resurrection of Jesus has great significance to us as believers. Paul explains that because of our spiritual union with Jesus by faith, death will not be the end for us! We who are united with Jesus by saving faith will be raised to eternal life (1 Cor. 15:22)!

Jesus' Commissioning His Disciples
Matthew 28:18-20

Before departing from earth to return to the Father in heaven, Jesus commissioned His disciples to take the good news ("gospel") of the message of salvation to the nations. This commissioning took place on "the mountain" in Galilee (Matt. 28:16). The definite article ("the") indicates that Jesus had a particular mountain in mind. Although Matthew's text doesn't name the specific mountain, the most prominent mountain in the vicinity of the Sea of Galilee is Mount Arbel from which travelers can enjoy a spectacular view of the Sea of Galilee.

I suggest it was there, on the summit of Mt. Arbel, overlooking the region where Jesus had concentrated His ministry, that He made a great claim: "All authority has been given to Me in heaven and on earth" (Matt. 28:18). Jesus has all power and the right to exercise it. It is on the basis of His absolute and complete authority that Jesus commissioned the eleven apostles as worldwide disciple makers.

The traditional translation of Matthew 28:19 is, "Go therefore and make disciples of all nations...." But the only imperative verb in the verse is "make disciples." The word "go" is a participle. The literal translation is, "As you are going, *make disciples*...." The *going* is assumed. The *commission* is to "make disciples." A disciple is a "learner." The ministry of making disciples is simply introducing people to Jesus and teaching them about who He is and the redemptive work He has accomplished.

Notice that the commission to "make disciples" is not limited to Judea or the land of Israel. Jesus charged the apostles to "make disciples of *all* the nations." The mission of carrying the good news to the nations is not a new idea being introduced by Jesus. It can be traced all the way back to God's promise to Abraham where the patriarch was told of God's plans to "bless all the families of the earth" (Gen. 12:3). Jesus commissioned the apostles to be a channel of blessing to the nations as they proclaimed the good news about His person and work.

Jesus instructed His apostles that two activities must accompany the mission of making disciples—baptism and teaching. *First*, those who believe are to be "baptized." This Greek word has been introduced into English translations without actually being translated. The word literally means to be "immersed." Immersion was an identification ritual which was part of the process of a Gentile becoming Jewish. The same tradition is now applied to those who were becoming followers of Jesus. They were to be immersed in water as a recognized means of embracing a new identification. By the ritual of immersion in water, they would now be *identified* as followers of Jesus.

Second, those who believe are to be taught what Jesus taught during his earthly ministry. Teaching is essential to disciple making. Those who become followers of Jesus must be instructed "to observe" all that Jesus taught. The word "observe" indicates that the curriculum for disciple making is not just doctrine, but practice. Disciple making involves instruction in doctrine with a view to personal and practical application.

In verse 20, Messiah Jesus promised that His followers won't have to do the job of disciple making alone. Jesus assures them of His spiritual presence until He returns at the end of the present age. It was prophesied that the virgin born Messiah of Isaiah 7:14 was to be called "Immanuel," meaning "God with us." Yet, Jesus was never called by this name. But He fulfills the *significance* of this name with the promise, "I am with you always, even until the end of the age" (Matt. 28:20).

Jesus' great commission is a continuation of God's plan to bring the blessings of salvation to all the nations of the earth. Have we joined hands with the apostles in embracing God's plan? Are we making disciples as we are going our different ways to various places on earth? While Jesus' "Great Commission" was addressed to His apostles, it has relevance today for each and every believer as they journey through life.

Jesus' Return to Heaven
Acts 1:9-11

The last key event in the life of Christ on earth is His return home to heaven—an event that was prophesied by Isaiah (Isa. 52:13) and anticipated by Jesus (Lk. 9:51).

All Christians celebrate Jesus' birth at Christmas, but many fail to acknowledge Jesus' ascension. Yet, this is a very important event. Jesus explained in His Upper Room Discourse that His return to the Father proves that He lived an unblemished life on earth (John 16:7-11). Because Jesus lived a holy and sinless life, God the Father was pleased to welcome Him back to His heavenly home. Jesus announced His ascension to His disciples on the day of His resurrection. He told the disciples gathered in the Upper Room, "Go to my brethren and say to them, 'I ascend to My Father and your Father, and My God and your God'" (Jn. 20:17).

The ascension of Jesus is recorded in Acts 1:9-11. Luke writes, "And after He had said these things, He was lifted up while they were looking on, and a cloud received Him out of their sight. And as they were gazing intently into the sky while He was going, behold two men in white

95

clothing stood beside them. They also said, 'Men of Galilee, why do you stand looking into the sky? This Jesus, who has been taken up from you into heaven, will come in just the same way as you have watched Him go into heaven.'"

Notice words that Luke uses to describe this event:

He was "lifted up" (v. 9)
A cloud "received Him out of their sight" (v. 9)
He was "taken up from you" (v. 11)
You watched him "go into heaven" (v. 11).

These references make it clear that Jesus was going home. But the angels announced that He is coming again—personally, physically and visibly. Christmas celebrates the birth of Jesus. The ascension celebrates His return to His heavenly home. But as we will see in the next chapter, there is so much more to the story.

So, what is Jesus doing *now* in heaven? The New Testament Scriptures reveal that Jesus is still at work. And He is keeping pretty busy!

Chapter 3

The Life of Christ in Heaven

My mother was born and raised in the little town of Dublin, Georgia. But like many women of her generation, she met and married a WWII naval officer. After the war, my mom and dad moved back to Dublin, her hometown, where mother expected to live the rest of her life. But my dad was from the state of Washington. He had left his college program to join the Navy. But with the war over, he wanted to finish his degree.

Our family moved to Seattle were my dad completed his studies in Forestry at the University of Washington. After graduation he was offered a job in the forest products industry and our family moved to Eugene, Oregon, where mom and dad lived for the rest of their lives. Although my mother lived most of her life in Oregon, she always regarded Georgia as her home.

With my dad's blessing she would gather my siblings together and take us by train to Georgia for a month during the summer. Mom loved to go home. She loved to see her family, her friends, and to eat Georgia peaches and watermelon. Travelers visiting Georgia sometimes complain about the heat and humidity; but not my mother. She loved to breathe the heavy, moist air and feel perspiration on her skin from the hot Georgia sun.

Georgia was such a part of my mother's life experience that we played the song, "Georgia on my mind," at her memorial service. For my mother, going to Georgia was going home.

Although Jesus lived His life on planet earth, this world was not His home. Jesus came from heaven and returned to heaven when His earthly ministry was finished. I wonder if Jesus enjoyed His return to heaven as much as my mother enjoyed going back to Georgia. Going back home to His Father's house must have been very special for Jesus.

In the previous chapter, we focused our attention on what Jesus did during his life on earth. In this chapter, we want to reflect on what Jesus is doing *now*, after His return home to heaven. Although Jesus' redemptive work was completed on earth, the Bible reveals that there are eight things that Jesus is doing for us *now* in heaven. I think you will be encouraged to know what Jesus is doing now as He enjoys being at home with His Father in heaven.

Jesus, Enjoying fellowship with His Father
Acts 1:9-11

The ascension of Jesus was covered in the previous chapter where the event was considered from the viewpoint of Jesus' disciples. Now we want to consider it from the viewpoint of Jesus Himself.

Before my father died, I loved to go home for visits. I enjoyed seeing and talking with him. I especially appreciated hearing his stories. As dad got older, it seems that he had more stories to tell about his youth, his career and his travel adventures. During our visits, I also savored wandering around our family home, looking at the rooms, furniture and pictures which elicited so many memories. Although our home now belongs to another family, I still like driving by and remembering the sixty years our family lived at 2615 Columbia Street.

Jesus announced His ascension on the day of His resurrection. He told Mary Magdalene, who was the first witness of the resurrection, "Go to my brethren and say to them, 'I ascend to My Father and your Father, and My God and your God'" (Jn. 20:17). Jesus' ascension constituted His return home to His heavenly Father. It must have been something He longed for after His thirty plus years of life on earth. The conversations, the fellowship, the joy of working together--all of this would continue as it had in eternity past. What joyous anticipation there must have been in the mind of the Father and Son as they looked forward to renewing their heavenly fellowship!

Jesus returned home to heaven with His earthly work fully accomplished. But what is Jesus doing now? Is Jesus just sitting around on His glorious throne? Not at all! The Bible reveals that Jesus is still very much engaged in God's kingdom work.

Jesus, Preparing a Place for His Followers
John 14:3

On the night before His crucifixion, Jesus shared a Passover Supper with His apostles. After the meal, Jesus told His apostles that He was going away (Jn. 13:33). This announcement brought an expression of concern from Peter. He had two questions. (1) "Where are you going?" and (2) "Why can't I come?"

Jesus explained to Peter that He was going away to prepare a place for His followers in heaven. Jesus assured Peter, and the rest of the apostles, that after a place had been prepared, He would return to earth and take His followers to be with Him in heaven. This promise reveals that Jesus is busy preparing a home in heaven for each of us!

The King James translation of verse 2 may give us the impression that Jesus is preparing each of us a heavenly "mansion." But the word is better translated "dwelling place" or apartment. In the biblical culture, the patriarch of the family would build a large home centered around a courtyard. The home was made up of apartments where the extended family would have a place to live in the father's house. In the first century Roman world, this was called an *insula*. What joy and fellowship there must have been for families living together in a shared villa with mom and dad, siblings, nieces and nephews. And so it will be in the heavenly home Jesus is preparing for us.

After His life on earth, Jesus returned to heaven to make ready our eternal home in the Father's house. We often refer to people who die as "going to heaven." This concept is best understood as going to dwell forever with Jesus in our Father's heavenly *insula*.

Jesus, Officiating as Priest in Heaven's Sanctuary
Hebrews 8:1-2

The high priests in ancient Israel represented the people before God. Moses' brother Aaron was Israel's first high priest. There were 83 high priests that officiated from

Aaron until the fall of Jerusalem in A.D. 70. Israel's high priests officiated at the altar during Israel's religious festivals.

On the Day of Atonement, the high priest would enter the Holy of Holies in the temple and place blood on the top of the ark of the covenant to cleanse the people of Israel from their past sins.

The high priests of Israel did a fairly good job at representing the people before God. But the writer of Hebrews insists that Jesus is a high priest who is better than any high priest in Israel's past (Heb.7:23-25). Jesus is a high priest who ministers in a better sanctuary! He carries out His ministry in a heavenly sanctuary, of which the earthly tabernacle is a "mere copy and shadow" (Heb. 8:5).

Jesus is a high priest who mediated a better covenant (Heb. 8:6). The covenant mediated by Moses at Mt. Sinai promised blessings for obedience, but provided no power for such obedience. The New Covenant mediated by Jesus at the cross promises the unconditional blessings of regeneration and forgiveness of sin through faith in Jesus (Heb. 8:10-12).

Jesus is also a high priest who offers a better sacrifice (Heb. 10:11-18). Animal sacrifices could only cleanse the flesh from ritual impurity and could never make the worshiper perfect before God. But Christ's sacrifice provides cleansing of the conscience and perfects, for all time, those who put their faith in His sacrifice (Heb. 9:13-14; 10:14). And while the animal sacrifices of the Old Covenant had to be repeated, the sacrifice Jesus made on the cross is sufficient for all time (Heb. 10:18). It never has to be repeated.

Because Jesus' sacrifice is for all time and never has to be repeated, Jesus "sat down at the right hand of God" (Heb. 10:12). You never read about the high priest in ancient Israel sitting down. There was no chair for the high priest in the tabernacle or temple. There was no chair because the high priest's work under the Old Covenant never ended. There was *always* another sacrifice, *always* another cleansing ritual, *always* more blood to sprinkle and incense to burn!

So, what is Jesus doing in heaven now? He is seated in a position of honor at the right hand of God because He has finished His redemptive work. What a blessing to know that our salvation is secure in the finished work of Jesus. The writer of Hebrews concludes, "Now where there is forgiveness of these things, there is no longer any offering for sin" (Heb. 10:18).

Jesus, Interceding for Believers
Hebrews 7:2

The fourth thing that Jesus is doing for believers in heaven is praying for us. In John 17 we find a prayer that Jesus prayed for His eleven disciples in the Upper Room. Jesus brought three requests before His Heavenly Father:

First, "Keep them in Your name" (v. 11).
Second, "Keep them from the evil one" (v. 15).
Third, "Sanctify them in the truth" (v. 17).

It is encouraging to know that Jesus is still praying for His followers. Although Jesus' sacrificial ministry has been completed, His intercessory ministry continues. The writer of Hebrews records that since Jesus holds his priesthood permanently, "He is able to save forever those who draw near to God through Him, since He always lives to make intercession for them" (Heb. 7:25). What an encouragement to know that Jesus is always praying for us.

My mother was a great prayer warrior. When I was a little boy and stricken with polio, my mother prayed all through the first night of my illness that God would spare my life and restore me to health. Throughout my youth and into my adult years, my mother continued to pray for me. She prayed for my ministry, for my marriage and for my children. One of the things I have missed since her death is the encouragement of knowing that my mom is praying for me.

But the writer of Hebrews tells us that the prayers of Jesus for His followers did not end at His death. Since Jesus was raised from the dead and is alive and well today, He continues to pray for us!

- ➢ Jesus prays for us when we are discouraged.
- ➢ Jesus prays for us when we are tempted to sin.
- ➢ Jesus prays for us when we need wisdom for big decisions.
- ➢ Jesus is always ready and willing to receive our requests and bring them before His Father in heaven.

With this in mind, the writer of Hebrews exhorts us with these words: "Let us draw near with confidence to the throne of grace, so that we may receive mercy and find grace to help in time of need" (Hebrews 4:16).

Jesus, Answering the Prayers of His People
John 14:13-14.

It is encouraging to know that Jesus is praying for His people. But it is even more heartening to know that because of His intercessory work, our prayers will be answered. Speaking to His disciples in the Upper Room, Jesus said, "Whatever you ask in My name, that will I do, so that the Father may be glorified in the Son. If you ask Me anything in My name, *I will do it*" (Jn. 14:13-14).

Here Jesus reveals the key to answered prayer. We must ask "in Jesus name." So what does it mean to pray "in Jesus name." In the time of Jesus, a person's name was more than a "name tag." People were often named or renamed after a significant character trait. Joseph was told that Mary's child would be named Jesus, which means "salvation." The angel then explains, "For He will save His people from their sins" (Matt. 1:21). The name "Jesus" represents all that He is—Savior, Lord, Messiah.

To pray in the name of Jesus is to appeal to the Father on the basis of Jesus' merits and influence as God's Son and our great high priest.

(1) Prayer in Jesus' name must be consistent with His character.
(2) Prayer in Jesus' name is presenting a prayer that Jesus would be willing to sign His name to.
(3) Praying in Jesus' name is praying according to God's will. It is like saying, "I ask this because it is what Jesus would want."

Sometimes I begin my prayers "in Jesus name" rather than using these words as a concluding formula. I open my prayer like this:

> "Heavenly Father, I come before your throne today in the strong and faithful name of Jesus. It is on the basis of His work as my sinless Savior that I bring my concerns before you. I believe this prayer is one that Jesus would pray for me and sign His name to."

Then, I go on to let my requests be known and thank God for hearing and answering *because of Jesus*.

Oregon Public Broadcasting has a phone-a-thon several times a year, appealing to viewers to help fund their broadcasts. After an hour of special entertainment, they take a break and announce, "Our phone lines are open and awaiting your call."

It is reassuring to know that heaven's phone line is always open. God wants to hear from His people. So we can simply close our eyes and speak to the Father saying, "This is Carl praying in the name of Jesus." And God the Father will be glad to "pick up" and answer!

Jesus, Defending Believers from Our Accuser
1 John 2:1-2)

During WWII my dad trained as a naval aviator and was assigned to fly his airplane over the Panama Canal to defend American interests against enemy sabotage. Nobody living in the United States during WWII doubted that we had an enemy who was seeking to destroy us.

105

Imperial Japan had bombed Pearl Harbor. German submarines were sinking American ships in the Atlantic. WWII ended in 1945, but we still have a *spiritual* enemy who is seeking to destroy us. We also have a strong defender in the person of Jesus Christ.

The apostle John writes, "My little children, I am writing these things to you so that you may not sin. And if anyone sins, we have an Advocate with the Father, Jesus Christ the Righteous One" (1 Jn. 2:1). The word translated "Advocate" is *paracletos*, literally "one called alongside for help." The word was used in legal contexts to refer to a "counsel for the defense." If you were arrested for a crime you didn't commit, you could hire an attorney who would go to court and present evidence of your innocence. Your attorney would defend you before your accusers. That is one of the things Jesus is doing presently in heaven. He is our advocate, our defender, our defense attorney in the celestial courtroom.

The prophet Zechariah had a vision of this kind of defense taking place in heaven. In his vision, Zechariah saw Israel's high priest standing before the Lord in robes that were spattered with filth. The high priest represented Israel, and his filthy garments depicted Israel's sin.

And standing at his side was Satan, the "accuser of our brethren" (Rev. 12:10). But as Satan began his accusations, the Lord spoke and said, "The Lord rebuke you Satan. Indeed, the Lord who has chosen Jerusalem rebuke you" (Zech. 3:2). Then the high priest's filthy garments were removed and he was clothed in festal robes.

Zechariah's vision is a beautiful picture of what Jesus

is doing in heaven as our defender. Satan loves to point out our sin and failure. He whispers in our ear, "You are a terrible Christian. Do you really think that Jesus loves someone like you? You are a sinner, not a saint. Do you really think that God is going to let someone like you into heaven?"

Our lack of faith may lead us to conclude that Satan is right! But then Jesus steps forward and before our Heavenly Father declares that all our sins and failures were paid for on the cross at "Scull Hill" (Golgotha). And because of the cross, we stand before God not as sinners, but as saints clothed in the righteousness of Christ. Don't let our enemy, Satan, deceive you into thinking that you just a lousy sinner. Because of the work of Jesus, you are a saint; and Jesus stands ready in heaven to defend you against Satan's lies and accusations.

Jesus, Ruling and Gifting His Church
Ephesians 4:10-12; 5:23-24,32

The seventh thing that Jesus is doing for us in heaven is ruling and gifting His church. The Apostle Peter tells us that Jesus is the "Chief Shepherd" of the church (1 Pet. 5:4). Paul describes Him as the "head of the church" (Eph. 5:23).

While there are many pastors, elders and various church leaders, there is just one CEO; and that's Jesus! Our Savior Jesus is the One who rules His church. He is the one to whom all church leaders must submit. But in addition to ruling the church, Jesus also provides gifted leaders for the church so that it can function effectively and reach its maximum potential.

In Ephesians 4:11, Paul writes that Jesus "gave some apostles, some prophets, some evangelists, some pastors and teachers."

The *apostles* were chosen by Jesus to be with Him and announce His resurrection.

The *prophets* spoke for God and communicated His special revelation.

The *evangelists* preach the gospel—the good news!

The *pastors* or *shepherds* care for the spiritual needs of God's flock.

The *teachers* remind people of the great truths about God and the person and work of Jesus.

These gifts are actually *gifted leaders* that are given to the church "for the equipping of the saints for the work of service, to the building up of the body of Christ" (Eph. 4:12). Paul goes on to explain that spiritual growth in the church will take place when these gifted leaders are doing their job.

The gifts of "apostle" and "prophet" were used to lay the foundation of the church (Eph. 2:20) and may have fulfilled their purpose in the first century. But God is still raising up evangelists, pastors and teachers for the work of the church today. It has been a privilege to have many of these gifted leaders in my classes during my career at

Western Seminary. And it is a blessing to see them fulfilling their calling as they serve Christ's body, the church.

Jesus, Receiving Worship from the Heavenly Court
Revelation 4:8-11

The book of Revelation tells us a great deal about the future. Many people believe that this book is primarily about prophecy. But while there is a great deal of prophecy in the book, the primary message of the book is about Jesus. The book of Revelation tells us of the glorious return, the final judgment and ultimate triumph of Jesus Christ.

In chapters 4 and 5, the book of Revelation shows us what is going on in heaven. John saw, in a vision, a door standing open into heaven and was invited to "Come up here" (Rev. 4:1). There in heaven, John saw someone seated on a throne, with 24 elders and four living creatures gathered around the throne in ceaseless worship.

John reports in his Revelation that, day and night, the heavenly creatures do not cease to say, "Holy, holy, holy is the Lord God, the Almighty, who was and who is and who is to come" (4:8).

John goes on to describe a "Lamb, standing as if slain," approached the throne to take a book from the hand of the one seated on the throne. When the Lamb took the book, the 24 elders fell down before Him singing, "Worthy are You to take the book and to break its seals; for You were slain and purchased for God, with Your blood, men from every tribe and tongue and people and nation" (Rev. 5:9).

Suddenly, John heard the voices of thousands and thousands of angels joining with the 24 elders saying, "Worthy is the Lamb that was slain to receive power and riches and wisdom and might and honor and glory and blessing" (Rev. 5:12). And the four living creatures kept saying, "Amen." And the 24 elders fell down and *worshiped* (Rev. 5:14).

Revelation 4-5 reveals the worship that Jesus is presently receiving in heaven. The angels and heavenly creatures are *declaring the worth* of Jesus and are demonstrating their *attitude* of worship by falling down before Him.

If the elders and angels and living creatures are worshiping Jesus in heaven now, what are the implications for us today? I think this suggests that we should be worshiping Him too! We can worship with our voices, our songs, our gifts, our service and even by our posture.

In addition to my grandparents and other more distant relatives, there are three members of my family now with Jesus in heaven—my mom and dad and my brother. I sometimes wonder what they are doing. I wonder if they know what I am doing here on earth. These are questions that the Bible doesn't answer. But we do know of at least eight things Jesus is doing right now in heaven.

(1) Jesus is enjoying fellowship with his Heavenly Father.
(2) Jesus is preparing a place in heaven for us.

110

(3) Jesus is officiating as priest in the heavenly
    sanctuary.
(4) Jesus is interceding for us before the Father.
(5) Jesus is hearing and answering our prayers.
(6) Jesus is defending us when Satan accuses and
    attacks.
(7) Jesus is ruling and gifting the church with
    leadership that helps us grow spiritually.
(8) Jesus is receiving worship from the angels and
    heavenly creatures.

While Jesus has finished His redemptive work on
earth, He didn't go into retirement. Because of His great
love, Jesus is continuing to work on our behalf in heaven.
What an encouragement to have this assurance from
God's Holy Word!

Chapter 4

The Life of Christ in Prophecy

The Bible tells us a great deal about what Jesus has done in the past and what He is doing in the present. Many sermons have been preached and books written on this subject. But what Jesus *will* do in the future is often either ignored or becomes the subject of much speculation. There is certainly a danger in trying to pinpoint the dates of events which are prophesied in the future. And yet, if we ignore what the Bible reveals about future events, we miss out on some very practical principles and great spiritual blessing.

What the Bible reveals about the future gives us *hope*. Jesus told His disciples, "In the world you have tribulation" (Jn. 16:33). He explains further that the unbelieving world will hate Jesus' followers and persecute them to the point of death (Jn. 15:18-20). It is not a happy prospect to be rejected, persecuted and possibly martyred by people who are hostile to God and those who have embraced Israel's promised Messiah. But the Bible doesn't leave us without hope. We gain hope and encouragement from God's promises about the future that God has planned for His people.

Biblical prophecy provides *encouragement* when we face trying circumstances (Jn. 14:1-3). Biblical prophecy provides *comfort* for grieving believers through the confidence that we will be united with our Christian loved ones again (1 Thess. 4:13-18). Biblical prophecy provides *motivation* to serve Christ and His church knowing that our earthly labors will reap heavenly rewards (1 Cor. 15:58). And finally, biblical prophecy provides a *reason and motivation* for personal purity, knowing that Jesus could return at any time (1 Jn. 3:2-3). We would not want to be found in a compromising situation when He arrives.

In this chapter you will discover nine things that Jesus will do in the future which are both practical and relevant for His followers today. Most importantly, your study of these events will give you hope. Paul's prayer in Romans 15:13 is my prayer for you. "Now, may the God of hope fill you with all peace in believing, so that you will abound in hope by the power of the Holy Spirit."

Jesus Will Meet Believers at the Rapture
1 Thessalonians 4:13-18

Jesus told His disciples that after completing His redemptive mission, He would return to the Father in heaven. But Jesus assured His followers that after preparing their heavenly home, He was coming again! Jesus said, "If I go and prepare a place for you, I will come again and receive you to Myself, that where I am, there you may be also" (Jn. 14:3). The return of Jesus for His followers is called the "rapture," taken from the word "caught up" (*arpazo*) in 1 Thessalonians 4:17. I believe that the rapture of Jesus' followers is the next great prophetic event revealed in Scripture.

The believers at Thessalonica were upset. They mistakenly thought that those who died before the Lord's return would miss out on it completely. Apparently confused by some false teaching, the Thessalonians had come to believe that the rapture was for the living believers only! In 1 Thess. 4:13-18 Paul writes to clarify the relationship between the living and the dead at the time of the rapture.

Paul relieves this concern in 1 Thess. 4:15 with words of assurance, "For this we say to you by the word of the Lord, that we who are alive and remain until the coming of the Lord, will not precede those who have fallen asleep." Paul explains in the next verse that the program of Jesus' return begins with the resurrection of the dead in Christ. "For the Lord Himself will descend from heaven with a shout, with the voice of the archangel and with the trumpet of God, and the dead in Christ will rise first" (1 Thess. 4:16).

After the dead believers are raised to meet Jesus at His return, then the living saints will follow. "Then we who are alive and remain will be caught up together with them in the clouds to meet the Lord in the air, and so we shall always be with the Lord" (1 Thess. 4:17).

Paul's point in this text is clear. The followers of Jesus who have died before His return will not miss out on the glorious return and reign of Christ. They will be the *first* to be raised! Then the living saints will follow. Notice the words in verse 17, "together with them." This means that the dead in Christ and the believers who are alive at the rapture will enjoy a glorious reunion! Have you missed your parents or grandparents, a sibling or a child, who has been separated from you by death? You will see them again! It is encouraging to know that believers will be united together again when Jesus returns. This is good news to those who have lost loved ones! Paul concludes this discussion, "Therefore, comfort one another with these words" (1 Thess. 4:18).

October 20, 2015, is a day I will never forget. It was that evening that my sister called to say that my dad had taken his last breath. Dad had been in decline since late summer. At the age of 92, we were not too surprised that he was approaching the end of his life. My sister, who had been giving him care since he was confined to bed, was there when he died. He simply told her, "thank you," closed his eyes and stopped breathing.

I miss my dad at every family birthday party and holiday celebration. But I am confident that I shall see him again on that great day when Jesus comes for His people and the dead in Christ are raised. Then we who are alive will be raptured from this earth and meet our loved ones in the clouds. What a wonderful family reunion that will be for the followers of Jesus.

Jesus Will Initiate the Tribulation Judgments
Revelation 5:1-7, 6:1

The book of Revelation reveals a great deal about what Jesus will do in the future. The book divides nicely into three sections based on instructions given to the Apostle John, "Therefore write the things which you have seen and the things which are and the things which will take place after these things" (Rev. 1:19). Chapters 4 and

116

5 form the prologue to the prophetic section of the book (Rev. 6-22).

Revelation 4 records John's vision of God sitting on His throne in heaven. Seated around God's throne are 24 elders, clothed in white with golden crowns on their heads. John reports that in addition to the 24 elders, there are four living creatures worshiping before God's throne. Day and night, they do not cease to proclaim, "Holy, holy, holy is the Lord God, the Almighty, who was and who is and who is to come" (Rev. 4:8). In response, the 24 elders fall down, casting their crowns before God's throne as an act of worship (Rev. 4:10), saying "Worthy are You, our Lord and our God, to receive glory and honor and power; for You created all things, and because of Your will they existed, and were created" (Rev. 4:11).

John continues describing his vision in Revelation 5. He calls our attention to a book sealed with seven seals in God's right hand. A strong angel asks with a loud voice, "Who is worthy to open the book and to break its seals?" Because no one responded and the question remained unanswered, John began to weep! Then one of the 24 elders speaks, "Stop weeping; behold, the Lion that is from the tribe of Judah, the Root of David, has overcome so as to open the book and its seven seals" (Rev. 5:5). The "Lion of Judah" is a messianic reference to Jesus (Gen. 49:8-10). He comes as the "root" or descendant of David (Matt. 1:1-17). Jesus is the one who has "overcome" death by His resurrection (Matt. 28:1-6). The resurrected Messiah, Jesus, is clearly the one who has authority to take God's book and break its seals.

In the next scene of his vision, John sees a Lamb (Jn. 1:29) approach God's throne and take the book from His right hand (Rev. 5:6-7). In response, the 24 elders, the living creatures, thousands and thousands of angels and all creation begin to worship, "To Him who sits on the throne, and to the Lamb, be blessing and honor and glory and dominion forever and ever" (Rev. 5:13).

The visions that follow reveal the contents of the sealed book. When each of the seven seals are broken, judgments come upon the earth from the throne of God (Rev. 6:1-8:1). The breaking of the seventh seal initiates another series of judgments—the trumpet judgments (Rev. 8:2-11:19). Again, the seventh trumpet judgement initiates seven bowl judgments (Rev. 16:1-21). The important thing to observe here is that the judgments of the tribulation are initiated by Jesus, who is not only the world's Savior, but also the world's Judge. Jesus Himself acknowledged this with His words, "For not even the Father judges anyone, but He has given all judgment to the Son... And He gave Him authority to execute judgment, because He is the Son of Man (Jn. 5:22-27, cf. Dan. 7:13).

Following the removal of the believers from the earth through the rapture, Jesus will initiate seven years of judgment referred to in Scripture as the "Tribulation" (Matt. 24:9, 21). While not all my friends would agree, I am persuaded that Christ will first come for His people (the *Rapture*) and then, after the seven-year Tribulation judgment, He will come with His angels (the *Return*) to set up the Messianic (Millennial) Kingdom. While the return of

Christ to this earth (usually referred to as the Second Coming) is heralded by many signs (cf. Matt. 24:4-26), the rapture is an event which is imminent. That is, it is unannounced and could occur at any moment (Tit. 2:13). After removing His people from the earth, Jesus will initiate the judgments of the Tribulation.

It is important to understand that the Tribulation judgments are not merely intended as judgements on sin, but are designed to lead unbelievers to repentance so that they can enter into God's provision of salvation which has been purchased and provided through the sacrificial death of Jesus (Acts 2:38; 4:12; 10:43; 16:31).

Jesus Will Return to Claim His Throne
Matthew 24:29-31; Revelation 19:11-16

Although Christians may differ on many of the prophetic details described in the Bible, together we embrace the doctrine of the Second Coming of Jesus. His first coming was at His birth in Bethlehem (Lk. 2:1-20). Jesus came first to redeem fallen humanity. But He will come again to judge the nations and rule Israel's promised kingdom.

Jesus spoke to His disciples about His Second Coming in the Olivet Discourse (Matt. 24-25). There He revealed that following the judgments of the Tribulation, He would be coming again. Jesus said, "For just as the lightning comes from the east and flashes even to the west, so will the coming of the Son of Man be. Wherever the corpse is, there the vultures will gather" (24:27-28).

Jesus was saying that His Second Coming will be sudden, clearly visible and accompanied by judgment. Jesus' return won't be a long-term process. It will be quick, like lightning. It won't be a hidden, secret event. Like lightning flashing in the night sky, people won't be able to miss the event. The accompanying judgment is suggested by the "corpse" and the gathering "vultures." In Scripture, divine judgment is symbolized by the presence of wild birds and beasts feeding on the bodies of the slain (Deut. 28:26). And so, as a corpse attracts hungry vultures, so open rebellion and unbelief will elicit God's judgment.

Jesus goes on to point out that the Tribulation period will be culminated by a darkness and cosmic chaos (Matt. 24:29). But then Jesus, Son of Man, will appear, "coming on the clouds of the sky with power and great glory" (Matt. 24:30). At that time, Jesus will send forth His angels to "gather together His elect" who will be invited into His kingdom (Matt. 24:31). The "elect" referred to here are those called by God during the Tribulation. These are the elect of Israel who have repented and turned to their Messiah during the Tribulation. Paul may have referred to this event when he wrote to the Romans, "And so all Israel will be saved; just as it is written, 'The Deliverer will come from Zion, He will remove ungodliness from Jacob. This is My covenant with them when I take away their sins'" (Rom. 11:26; Isa. 59:20-21). The repentant people of Israel will then be gathered and ushered into their long awaited messianic kingdom (Zech. 10:9-12; Ezek. 20:37-38; 37:1-14).

Further insight into Jesus' Second Coming is found in Revelation 19:11-16. The book of Revelation focuses our attention on Jesus and His Second Coming. John's visions announce that Jesus is coming again, in power, in glory and in judgment. Following the events of Tribulation (Rev. 6-18), John hears a fourfold "Hallelujah" announcing the return of Jesus to reign and rule over His prophesied, messianic kingdom (Rev. 19:1-6). The traditional Jewish marriage supper is used as a metaphor of the preparation and celebration of the imminent union of the Bride (true believers) with the Bridegroom (King Jesus).

John goes on to describe his vision of Jesus' return on a white horse to judge and wage war (Rev. 19:11). His robe is "dipped in blood," perhaps His own blood which Jesus shed for sin (Eph. 2:13) or the blood of His enemies (Rev. 14:19-20). Jesus will be accompanied at His return by the angelic "armies which are in heaven" which follow Him on white horses (Rev. 19:14; Mk. 8:38). The announcement of coming judgment in Rev. 19:11 is elaborated in verse 15. "From His mount comes a sharp sword, so that with He may strike down the nations." The "nations" refers to the enemy nations which have gathered around Jerusalem in order to destroy the Holy City and prevent Jesus from taking His rightful, messianic throne (Zech. 14:2-4).

John's vision of Jesus' return assures us that the unbelieving world's opposition to His return will be unsuccessful. Jesus will "strike down the nations, and He will rule them with a rod of iron" (Rev. 19:15; Psa. 2:8-9). On the day of Jesus' return, there will be no doubt about who rules the world, for on His robe and on His thigh are the words, "King of Kings and Lord of Lords" (Rev. 19:16)!

Nobody knows--not even the angels in heaven--when Jesus will return to claim His crown and His promised throne. But at the end of the book of Revelation, Jesus Himself told the Apostle John, "I am coming quickly" (Rev. 22:20). And we, as Jesus' followers, join John in responding, "Amen! Come, Lord Jesus."

Jesus Will Rule His Promised Kingdom
Revelation 20:1-6

Immediately after His Second Coming, Jesus will execute judgment on the "beast" and "false prophet" who led the earthly rulers in opposing His return. They will be seized and "thrown alive into the lake of fire which burns with brimstone" (19:20). But what about Satan who instigated humanity's initial rebellion (Gen. 3:1-6) and has continually challenged God's claim for world dominion? John was given a vision of Satan's confinement in a tightly sealed "abyss" for a period of one-thousand years (Rev. 20:2-3).

With Satan and his associates judged and confined, Jesus will be unopposed as He assumes the throne of David in the city of Jerusalem (2 Sam. 7:12-16). But Jesus won't rule alone. John reports that the believers who lost their lives during the seven-year Tribulation period will be resurrected to reign with Jesus for one-thousand years (Rev. 20:4-6). Many Bible scholars have questioned whether the "thousand-years" should be understood literally or figuratively. Is the Revelation referring to a specific period of time or simply giving us a metaphor which describes a period of long duration? There is much in the book of Revelation that is symbolic. But the number "one-thousand" is mentioned *six* times! It is best to assume that the number is literal unless there is something in the immediate text or parallel passages that would deter us from this conclusion. The important thing to appreciate in this text is that there *will be* a future reign of Jesus which He will share with those who have loved and served Him.

The *future* rule and reign of Jesus is a major theme of biblical prophecy (cf. 2 Sam. 7:12-16; Lk. 1:32-33; 1 Cor. 15:25-26; Phil. 2:9-11). But some theologians will say that Jesus is *already* reigning from heaven, and I would readily agree. There is biblical evidence that Jesus is reigning today (Lk. 17:21, Col. 1:13). But the present rule of Jesus from heaven does not fulfill the biblical prophecies regarding Jesus' rule over the nations from David's throne in Jerusalem. I suggest that the kingdom of God is a *present* spiritual reality which has a *future* culmination. Yes, there is a present, spiritual reign of Jesus from heaven. His present, heavenly reign will be culminated at Jesus' return by His physical, earthly reign over the nations.

You may be wondering what the future kingdom reign of Jesus will be like. The people of Israel anticipated a future kingdom and the prophets told them what this time would be like. Here is a short list of kingdom promises:

- ➤ Peace will prevail. There will be no war in God's kingdom (Isa. 2:4).
- ➤ God will reign over Jerusalem. People will come from the surrounding nations to worship Him there (Isa. 2:3, Joel 3:1).
- ➤ Justice and righteousness will prevail in government and throughout the land (Isa. 9:7).
- ➤ Agriculture will flourish. There will be no lack of food in God's kingdom (Amos 9:13).
- ➤ There will be no physical infirmity or handicaps. No one will be blind, deaf, lame or mentally handicapped (Isa. 35:5-6).
- ➤ The people of Israel will be safe and secure in Israel--their promised land (Amos 9:14-15; Ob. 19-21).

You can imagine how the people of Israel longed for the coming of God's kingdom. We join them in this blessed hope of Jesus' return to rule and reign over His messianic kingdom.

Jesus Will Judge Satan and His Followers
Revelation 20:7-10

The next event in the unfolding prophetic timeline is Satan's release from his thousand-year confinement. John records, "When the thousand years are completed, Satan will be released from his prison and will come out to deceive the nations which are in the four corners of the earth...to gather them together for war" (Rev. 20:7-8). While only believers will enter Jesus' messianic kingdom, it appears that there will be people born during that period who will have to make a decision for or against Christ. Many will place their faith in Jesus, but others will harbor rebellion against God in their hearts. At the end of the thousand years, they will be given a chance to show their true allegiance.

Released from the abyss, Satan will gather his followers for one final war against Jesus and God's people in Jerusalem, "the beloved city" (Rev. 20:9). The cosmic conflict between God and His enemy, Satan, will end abruptly as fire descends from heaven, destroying the followers of Satan as they besiege Jerusalem. Then Satan, the deceiver of God's people, will be "thrown into the lake of fire and brimstone" to join his associates, the beast and false prophet. There the enemies of God and His people will be tormented day and night forever (Rev. 20:10). At this point in the world's future history, all wicked opposition to God has been brought under the Messiah King's authority. The head of the serpent has been crushed (Gen. 3:15). Jesus will now reign unopposed over His creation and kingdom forever.

Jesus Will Officiate at the Final Judgment
Revelation 20:11-15

Following Jesus' final victory over Satan and His followers (Rev. 20:7-10), the unbelieving dead will be raised and judged. You might be wondering, "Wasn't there a resurrection at the time of the rapture?" Yes, indeed. But the Bible teaches that there will be a resurrection of the

125

believers, followed later by the resurrection of unbelievers. Jesus referred to these two resurrections in His teaching about eternal life. John recorded His words, "Do not marvel at this; for an hour is coming, in which all who are in the tombs will hear His voice and will come forth; those who did good deeds to a resurrection of life, those who committed evil deeds to a resurrection of judgment (Jn. 5:29-29). The resurrection to life takes place in two stages. The first stage takes place at the rapture of the church (1 Thess. 4:16-17). The second stage occurs at Jesus' return when the Old Testament saints and tribulation martyrs are raised (Dan. 12:2; Matt. 24:31; Rev. 20:4).

The resurrection described in Revelation 20:11-15 is the resurrection of the wicked, unbelieving dead. They might have assumed that by rejecting Jesus, they would simply be excluded from heaven. That would be bad enough. But it gets worse! The wicked, unbelieving dead will be raised from their graves to join their master, Satan, in the lake of fire. John records that the dead are judged "according to their deeds" (Rev. 20:13). How can this be reconciled with the biblical teaching that salvation comes as a free gift, apart from one's personal righteousness or good works?

John reveals that the books are opened and each person's record is examined and evaluated. The Bible teaches that we have all sinned and fallen short of God's righteous standard (Rom. 3:9-18,23). So what is recorded in the books isn't good! Then "the book of life" is consulted to see if one's failings and wicked deeds have been covered by the blood of Jesus. Is a person's name present or absent? It is the absence of a person's name in the "book of life" that determines their eternal destiny in the lake of fire. John describes the lake of fire as "the second death." Death separates the physical body from life on planet earth. The "second death" separates unbelieving people from God forever.

I believe that Revelation 20:15 is the saddest verse in the Bible. John writes, "And if anyone's name was not found written in the book of life, he was thrown into the lake of fire." This verse is sad because it describes the eternal destiny of those who reject God's provision of salvation in the Messiah. The sad and sobering fact is that those who reject God's offer of salvation through the redeeming work of Jesus will spend eternity in the place called hell. This hard truth is super sad because it doesn't have to be that way for *anyone*. Through Jesus' sacrificial death on the cross, God has provided a salvation that delivers us from the eternal consequences of sin and is sufficient for *all* who believe (Jn. 3:16; 5:24).

As we consider the sobering reality of eternal separation from our good, creator God, I want to emphasize that people don't go to hell because they are wicked. We are all wicked and undeserving of salvation. People go to hell because they have rejected God's provision of salvation. Their eternal destiny is based on a choice they have made. While God is sovereign over our lives and destinies (Rom. 8:28), He does not force people to get saved by trusting Jesus. A choice must be made.

Revelation 20:15 reveals just how eternally significant is the choice we all must make.

Jesus Will Comfort and Bless His People
Revelation 21:1-4

Having judged sinners and Satan, God will purge away the damage done by sin to His creation. A cleansing by fire will prepare the earth for eternity (Isa. 65:17; 66:22; 2 Pet. 3:10-13).

John's next vision describes the New Jerusalem where believers in Jesus will enjoy God's comfort and blessing forever (Rev. 21:1). This is the place that Jesus promised to prepare for His followers. Jesus told His disciples, "In my Father's house are many dwelling places; if it were not so, I would have told you; for I go to prepare a place for you" (Jn. 14:2). What John will describe in Revelation 21:1-22:5 is what most people refer to as "heaven." Here, through John's vision, the curtain of heaven is drawn back to give believers a foretaste of the glories to come.

What is heaven like? I believe that John's vision in Revelation 21:1-22:5 gives us the best picture of what heaven will be like for those who have placed their faith in the saving work of Messiah Jesus. John begins by describing the descent of a heavenly city, the New Jerusalem (Rev. 21:1-2). The city is identified as a "bride," adorned and prepared for her husband, Christ (Eph. 5:31-33). The imagery of the marriage between Christ and His followers indicates that this city is the residence of the followers of Jesus. This is the place that Jesus left earth to prepare as an eternal home for believers (Jn. 14:2-3).

John describes the New Jerusalem as a place where God dwells with his people (Rev. 21:3). There God will comfort and bless His people. John writes that God "will wipe away every tear from their eyes; and there will no longer be any death; there will no longer be any mourning, or crying, or pain (Rev. 21:4). All the suffering that came as a result of sin and characterized original creation will "have passed away." Since God will be "making all things new" (Rev. 21:5), all the suffering, pain and shame that came as a result of sin will be gone forever!

Who is going to live in this city and enjoy its blessings? John answers that question in Revelation 21:7. He writes, "He who overcomes will inherit these things and I will be his God and he will be My son." John uses the term "overcomer" in Revelation 2-3 to describe believers who are associated with the seven churches. In 1 John 5:5, the apostle John writes, "Who is the one who overcomes the world, but he who believes that Jesus is the Son of God?" The joys and blessings of the New Jerusalem are reserved for followers of Jesus, in contrast to unbelievers who will spend their eternity in the lake of fire (Rev. 21:8).

John goes on to describe the New Jerusalem. He tells us of its walls and gates. The gates are named for the twelve tribes of Israel while the foundation stones are named for the twelve apostles (Rev. 21:11-14). This clearly reveals that the New Jerusalem will be the eternal residence of the Old Testament saints (like Abraham,

Isaac and Jacob) as well as New Testament believers (like Paul, James and Barnabas). There will be one, *united* family of God living together in the New Jerusalem.

John even provides us with the dimensions of the city (Rev. 21:15-17). The angel measures the city and reports that the New Jerusalem is "fifteen hundred miles" in length, width and height. Whether the city will be in the shape of a square or a pyramid, the main point is clear. There will be no housing shortage in the New Jerusalem. There is plenty of room for all who believe. In addition to giving us the physical dimensions of the city, John tells us about the building materials. The city won't be made of concrete and asphalt, but of jasper, pure gold and precious stones.

The dimensions of the New Jerusalem and the description of its streets of gold have led some to conclude that this text should be understood figuratively, rather than literally. But there is nothing in the text which suggests this conclusion. The description of the city walls (21:12), streets (21:21), plants (22:2) and people (22:3) all point to a literal understanding. Jesus promised to prepare a place for God's people (Jn. 14:2-3) and it is completely within the realm of reason that He would want to describe it for us.

John concludes his description of the New Jerusalem by telling us about life in the city (Rev. 21:22-22:5). In contrast to Israel's past history, there will be no temple in the New Jerusalem (21:22). No worship center will be needed there, for the residents will have direct access to God the Father and the Lamb. The city won't need street lamps, sun, moon or stars, for it will be illuminated by the glory of God (21:23-24). The gates of the city will never be closed, for Satan and all of God's enemies will be confined to the lake of fire (21:25-26). There won't be a crime problem in the city because "no one who practices abomination and lying shall ever come into it, but only those whose names are written in the Lamb's book of life" (Rev. 21:27).

Perhaps you have wondered if we will need to *eat* in heaven. The beginning of the next chapter (Rev. 22) gives us a clue. The curse which came as a result of Adam and Eve's sin in the garden will be lifted (Rom. 8:20-22) and the trees in the New Jerusalem will bear their fruit year round (Rev. 22:1-3a). While our glorified, resurrected bodies won't *need* physical nourishment, eating is associated with fellowship and conversation around the table as well as the pleasure of tasting delicious food. I suggest that we will be able, if we wish, to eat in the New Jerusalem. Just think of enjoying fresh peaches and strawberries twelve months out of the year!

John's vision of the New Jerusalem reveals that heaven is a beautiful place where believers will enjoy fellowship with Jesus, rest, joy, peace and good food! What an abundant, eternal life awaits us!

Jesus Will Reverse the Curse of Sin
Revelation 22:3a

Looking back to the earliest beginnings recorded in Genesis, we see that God had a plan to bless His

131

creation. Three times in Genesis 1-2 we find the phrase, "God blessed" (Gen. 1:22,28; 2:3). But when Adam and Eve sinned by disobeying God's instructions to not eat of the tree of the knowledge of good and evil, a curse fell upon the earth. Three times in Genesis 3-4 we find the word "cursed" (Gen. 3:14,17; 4:11). But God was not willing to leave His creation, and the people who occupied it, in the mess they had brought about as a result of sin. So God began a plan to reverse the effects of the curse and restore blessing to His creation.

God intervened, at a time when sin reached a terrible climax, to spare Noah and his family from the consequences of humanity's sin. After a devastating judgment through a worldwide flood, God "blessed" Noah and his family (Gen. 9:1). Ten generations and 400 years later, God "blessed" Abraham and promised that Abraham's descendants would be a blessing to all the nations of the earth (Gen. 12:2-3). The promise of God's plan to restore world blessing was passed on to Abraham's son Isaac, his grandson Jacob and to his great-grandson Judah. It seems that God is pretty serious about restoring blessing to the sin-cursed earth!

The prophet Jeremiah advances the theme of blessing by announcing that a day would come when God would enact a New Covenant with His people which will replace the covenant they broke, resulting in disaster and death (Jer. 31:31-34). This New Covenant would focus on the internalization of God's law which will enable His people to obey His instructions and enjoy His blessing (Ezek. 36:25-27).

God's promise of restored blessing came to a climactic culmination when Jesus took humanity's sin upon Himself and bore divine wrath as a sacrificial substitute for all of our failings and sin. The writer of Hebrews declares that a new and better covenant has been established through the atoning work of Jesus (Heb. 8:6). The Old Covenant promised *blessings* for obedience, but didn't provide the internal (spiritual) empowerment to obey. The New Covenant promises unconditional *blessings* for all who will receive the gift of salvation which Jesus accomplished by His death on the cross. These blessings include the forgiveness of sin, the law written on our hearts, the indwelling and empowering ministry of the Holy Spirit and the blessing of enjoying a relationship with God as His people.

But wait! There is more! Although God had made provision for the restoration of blessing on humanity through the person and work of Jesus, a curse remains on His creation. Paul acknowledged this in his letter to the Romans. Paul explains that the creation was "subjected to futility" and exists today in "slavery to corruption" (Rom. 8:20-21). As a result of the curse which came through sin, "the whole creation groans and suffers the pains of childbirth together until now" (Rom. 8:22). But one day, this sin cursed creation is going to be "set free from its slavery to corruption into the freedom of the glory of the children of God" (Rom. 8:21).

That brings us to the new creation which God promised through the prophet Isaiah (Isa. 65:17; 66:22) and revealed to the Apostle John in the apocalyptic vision recorded in Revelation 21. God promised that the present creation, with all its pollution, corruption and damage resulting from the curse, will be purged, purified and made new (cf. 2 Pet. 3:7). Then, and only then, will God's great plan to restore blessing to His creation be complete. Finally, as John climatically declares, "THERE WILL NO LONGER BE ANY CURSE" (Rev. 22:3).

Removing the curse of sin from this earth is God's great plan for the ages! This plan is going to be fully accomplished through the person and work of Jesus who declared, "Behold, I am making all things new" (Rev. 21:5).

Jesus Will Welcome Eternal Worship and Service
Revelation 22:3b-4

I enjoy work. I enjoy working in my garden, remodeling my house and restoring my military jeeps. It is hard for me to imagine, let alone anticipate, an eternity without work. Will there be time and place in the New Jerusalem for work?

Some people have wondered if heaven might be boring because there won't be much to do. I don't think Jesus would prepare a heavenly home for His followers that was going to be *boring!* Revelation 22:3b helps us with this question. John records that God's bondservants (i.e. the believers) "will serve Him." This text reveals that the citizens of heaven will have the privilege of *serving* God throughout eternity. Paul supports this idea with his comment in 2 Timothy 2:12, "If we endure, we will also reign with Him." Endurance in the faith is the distinguishing mark of true believers. Paul is saying that believers will actually share in Jesus' kingdom reign! We are not told what our job descriptions will be, but I feel confident that the work God assigns us won't be boring.

What blessed fellowship we will enjoy as we serve God in His presence! John adds that believers will "see His face," no doubt a reference to the face of Jesus who returned to heaven in His resurrected, glorified body. Working together with Jesus as we serve the God of all creation is a joyous, future prospect! This is the ultimate blessing and eternal destiny of God's people.

Part 2

What Jesus Says

So far in *The Story of Jesus* we have focused our study on what Jesus *did*, is *doing* and *will do* in the future. But in this section of the book we will turn our attention to what Jesus *said* about a number of important and practical topics. In His final words before returning to the Father in heaven, Jesus instructed the eleven apostles to teach their disciples "to observe all I commanded you" (Matt. 28:20). Notice that word "observe." This indicates that Jesus didn't want His disciples just to know a lot of information, but to respond in obedience to what they had learned. This is what James had in mind when he wrote, "But prove yourselves to be doers of the word, and not merely hearers" (Jms. 1:22). As a follower of Jesus, you will find Jesus' teachings helpful as you plan your response to various situations you will probably encounter in your personal and spiritual life.

About Accountability

In their popular folk song, Simon and Garfunkel sang, "I've built walls, a fortress deep and mighty, that none may penetrate. I have no need of friendship, friendship causes pain. It's laughter and it's loving I disdain. I am a rock. I am an island" (1972). Some people have tried to live such an isolated and lonely existence, but it doesn't work for a follower of Jesus. The Christian life cannot be lived in isolation from the believing community. This is quite evident from the words of Jesus who commanded His disciples to hold each other accountable for their spiritual lives and behavior.

The classic text on spiritual accountability is found in Matthew 18:15-17 where Jesus explained four steps in confronting and correcting a faltering believer. The *first* step is to lovingly confront the brother or sister. "If your brother sins, go and show him his fault in private; if he listens to you, you have won your brother" (Matt. 18:15). Sadly, many Christians either ignore a brother or sister's spiritual failings or they speak (gossip) to someone else about it. Jesus teaches us to care enough to confront, correct and assist a struggling Christian. If the brother or sister responds positively, the matter should go no further. But if they brush off the correction, ignoring the issue of spiritual concern, Jesus instructed His disciples to take a *second* step. "But if he does not listen to you, take one or two more with you, so that by the mouth of two or three witnesses every fact may be confirmed" (Matt. 18:16). The witnesses increase the sphere of accountability and demonstrate that they share a concern for the spiritual failings. If the brother or sister persists in sinful behavior and refuses to be spiritually accountable, Jesus instructs that a *third* step of spiritual discipline must be taken. "If he refuses to listen to them, tell it to the church" (Matt. 18:17). Jesus taught that a brother or sister's sin is a matter of concern for the church family. Caring Christians are obligated to bring spiritual needs and failings before the community for prayer and increased accountability. The purpose is not to judge, embarrass or harass the sinner, but to show them genuine *agape* love by helping the floundering brother or sister face the issue of persistent sin and, by God's redeeming grace, to be delivered. It is so encouraging when a brother or sister acknowledges a spiritual problem and is willing to receive counsel and help.

The *fourth* step in spiritual accountability is to no longer regard the unrepentant, persistently sinning brother or sister as a member of the spiritual community. Only God knows for sure the condition of someone's heart, but when a person's actions clearly contradict their profession of faith, they cannot be regarded as a follower of Jesus or member of the Christian community.

The four steps of spiritual accountability set forth by Jesus encompass God's *loving* plan for restoring sinning saints to fellowship with Himself and each other in the body of Christ. You can't follow these steps as a "Lone Ranger," in isolation from the church and its leadership. It takes a community to hold one another accountable and help with the ministry of spiritual restoration. For further study on this important subject, see my book, *Your Guide to Church Discipline* (Bethany House, 1985).

About Anxiety

Are you prone to worry about things in life that you can't control? Perhaps you worry about your job security, your retirement account, your mortgage payments or your physical health? There is a great deal of uncertainty in life; and uncertainty often fills our hearts with anxiety. We worry about problems we have yet to face and we wonder, "Is everything going to be OK?"

In his Sermon on the Mount (Matthew 5-7), Jesus addressed the problem of our propensity toward anxiety. In fact, He mentioned this condition five times in Matthew 6:25-34. Jesus began by saying, "Stop worrying! Stop worrying about all the things you need for life" (Matt. 6:25). He pointed out that worry and anxiety will get you nowhere (Matt. 6:27). Jesus then offered three illustrations of how God meets the physical needs of His creatures. He feeds the birds of the air, clothes the lilies with glory, and beautifies the grass of the field. Arguing from the lesser to the greater, Jesus explained that if God cares for the birds and the plants (of lesser importance), He will most certainly provide for all the needs of His people (of greater importance)!

Instead of worrying about tomorrow's needs, Jesus exhorted His disciples to focus on kingdom priorities. "But seek first His kingdom and His righteousness." Then Jesus offered the assurance that when we give our attention to these spiritual priorities, "all these things will be added to you" (Matt. 6:33). The Apostle Peter may have had Jesus' teaching about anxiety in mind when he wrote, "Casting all your care on Him, because He cares for you" (1 Pet. 5:7).

About the Church

As important as the church is in the lives of God's people today, Jesus mentioned it just twice. In Matthew 16:18, Jesus promised, "I will build my church." In Matthew 18:17, Jesus instructed his disciples to "tell it to the church." What did Jesus have in mind when He used the word "church"?

Most people use the word "church" to refer to a building where Christians gather for worship, as in the question, "Where do you go to church?" But the Greek word translated "church" (*ekklesia*) actually refers to a *congregation*. A church is a congregation or assembly of people who have professed faith in Jesus as their sin-bearer and Savior. In the first century, the concept of the church was that of a congregation or gathering of people who had embraced Jesus as Israel's promised Messiah.

When Jesus promised to build His church, He was promising to gather His followers into a believing congregation. Paul later explained to the Ephesian believers that Jesus is the head of the church, "which is His body" (Eph. 1:22-23; 5:23). The church is not a building, but a congregation of Jesus' followers who submit to His leadership and authority and hold one another mutually accountable for their spiritual life and discipline.

About Compassion

Jesus was often moved by His compassion to respond to the needs of hurting and suffering people (Matt. 9:36; 14:14; 20:34). Before miraculously feeding the multitude, Jesus said, "I feel compassion for the people, because they have remained with Me now three days and have nothing to eat; and I do not want to send them away hungry, for they might faint on the way" (Matt. 15:32). In the parable of the prodigal son, Jesus told of how the father saw his son at a distance, "and felt compassion for him, and ran and embraced him and kissed him" (Lk. 15:20). In the gospels, *compassion* is one of the primary

141

motivations for Jesus to reach out and meet the needs of hurting people. This shouldn't surprise us.

When God revealed His glorious attributes to Moses (Exod. 34:6-8), the first thing He said about Himself was that He was "compassionate." Compassion is the tender, inward feeling of sympathetic concern that moves people to respond and help someone in need. Jesus incarnated and exemplified God's compassion throughout His life and ministry.

When the Pharisees accused Jesus' disciples of violating some of the Jewish traditions which had accumulated around the Sabbath law, Jesus defended His followers by quoting from the prophet Hosea. Jesus said, "If you had known what this means, 'I desire compassion, and not sacrifice,' you would not have condemned the innocent" (Hos. 6:6; Matt. 12:7). While the disciples were innocent of breaking the Sabbath, the Pharisees were ignorant of the Christ-motivating virtue of compassion. May we not be so ignorant today!

About Discipleship

Contrary to popular understanding, a disciple (Greek, *mathetes*) is not the same thing as a "believer." A disciple is a "interested learner" who *may* become a believer. But not all disciples are believers. We read of how some "disciples" who had heard Jesus' preaching and witnessed His miracles eventually turned away from following Jesus (Jn. 6:66). They had heard enough of Jesus' teaching and were not interested in embracing Him as Israel's Messiah. The imperative in the "Great Commission" (Matt. 28:19-20) is not, "Go into all the

142

world," but rather, "Make disciples of all the nations" (Matt. 28:19). As they journey through life, Jesus wants His followers to be disciple makers.

We often read in the Gospels of how Jesus withdrew with His disciples to a remote place to *spend time* with them (cf. Mk. 3:7). Mark writes, "And He appointed twelve, so that they would *be with Him* and that He could send them out to preach" (Mk. 3:14). John 3:22 records, "After these things Jesus and His disciples came into the land of Judea, and there He was *spending time with them* and baptizing." There appears to be two key factors in Jesus' pattern for discipleship. The first is "companionship." Jesus didn't just set up a classroom in the synagogue to train his disciples. He spent time with them, walking from village to village, eating meals together, going to weddings and funerals, attending Shabbat services at local synagogues, visiting the temple in Jerusalem and asking and answering questions.

The second key factor in discipleship is "instruction" in the words and works of Jesus. In His "great commission," Jesus instructed His apostles to teach their disciples "to observe all that I commanded you" (Matt. 28:20). Note that the *teaching* is with a view to *doing*. Discipleship is not simply instruction, but includes the practical application of instruction.

Considering the two essential ingredients to discipleship (companionship and instruction), I define discipleship as "personal companionship in preparation for spiritual leadership." Jesus didn't want His followers to sit around waiting for the inauguration of His future kingdom. He commanded them to be disciple makers, spending time with people who were interested in Jesus, sharing the gospel (the good news), teaching them what Jesus taught and helping them become true believers so they could be disciple makers too.

About Demons

The words "demon" and "demons" appear 54 times in the Gospels. There was a surge of demonic activity in connection with the life and ministry of Jesus. That was a time of great conflict between truth and error, light and darkness, belief and unbelief. And while this conflict continues today, the battle turned when Satan was defeated at the cross. We don't need to live today in fear of demons or their influence. Yet we must be vigilant and alert so that we do not fall prey to their deception.

Because demons are spirit beings without physical bodies (Rev. 16:14), they may seek out the physical body of a person or beast to manifest themselves (Mark 5:9-13). People in this condition are said to have an "unclean spirit" (Matt. 12:43; Mk. 1:23) or "the spirit of an unclean demon" (Lk 4:33). According to Jesus, demons are under the authority of Satan, "the ruler of the demons" (Matt. 12:24). They assist the evil one in attempting to thwart God's work in the lives of people. People who come under the deceptive influence of demons are described in the gospels as becoming "demonized" (*daimonizomai*).

Jesus frequently confronted demons, delivering people from their evil influence. The gospels record Jesus' encounter with a naked, demonized man living in tombs. The demons recognized Jesus, fell down before Him and cried out, "What business do we have with each other, Jesus, Son of the Most High God? (Lk. 8:28). Asserting His divine authority, Jesus commanded the demons and they departed. When people from a nearby village heard what had happened, they came and saw the demonized man sitting at the feet of Jesus, clothed and in his right mind (Lk. 8:35). As followers of Jesus, we proclaim that our Savior triumphed over demons by His death. And while they may tempt and deceive us, demons have no claim or rightful power over our lives today.

About His Deity

Some students of the gospels admire the teachings and ethics of Jesus, but deny His deity. They say that Jesus was a "good man," but that He was not God. I have wondered how Jesus could be considered a "good man" or an "ethical teacher" if He wrongly and deceitfully claimed to be God!

There is no doubt that Jesus claimed to be God. In John 10:30, Jesus said, "I and the Father are one." During His last evening with the apostles in the Upper Room, Jesus told Philip, "He who has seen Me has seen the Father" (Jn. 14:9). Even Jesus' enemies recognized Jesus' claim to deity, but rejected it. They angrily accused Him of blasphemy, saying, "You, being a man, make Yourself out to be God" (Jn. 10:33). The Apostle John supported Jesus' claim to deity with the first verse of his gospel, "In the beginning was the Word and the Word was with God, and the Word was God." In the person of Jesus, eternal God took on humanity to offer Himself as the ultimate sacrifice for the sins of the world. This is a truth that is beyond complete comprehension. But we believe it and thank God for it!

About Divorce

Jesus had some strong words to say about God's intended plan for marriage. After responding to the Pharisees' question about whether it was lawful for a man to divorce his wife, Jesus said, "What therefore God has joined together, let no man separate" (Mk. 10:9, Matt. 19:6). The emphasis of the Greek text is, "Stop separating what God has united in the marriage union." Jesus clearly taught that the marriage union was designed by God to be a permanent relationship, unbroken except by death.

Divorce and remarriage was accepted in Jewish tradition according to the rabbis' reading of Deuteronomy 24:1-4. But Jesus appealed to God's original plan for marriage in Genesis 2:24 to give His disciples four reasons why the marriage union should be regarded as permanent. *First*, divorce was not part of God's original plan for marriage. He made *one* female for *one* male (Mk. 10:6). *Second*, marriage was designed as the strongest of human relationships. "For this reason a man shall leave his father and mother and be joined to his wife" (Mk. 10:7). *Third*, in the marriage relationship, two people are united into *one* partnership. "And the two shall become one flesh; so they are no longer two, but one flesh" (Mk. 10:8). *Fourth*, divorce separates the union that "God has joined together" in marriage (Mk. 10:9).

Although Jesus answered the Pharisees question rather definitively, His disciples wondered about why

Moses appeared to have allowed divorce in Deuteronomy 24:1-4. Jesus explained that the Old Testament allowance for divorce was because of the "hardness" of the Israelite's hearts (Matt. 19:8) as demonstrated by their refusal to embrace God's plan for the permanence of marriage. But Jesus pointed out that it wasn't this way "from the beginning" (Matt. 19:8). Rather than focusing on possible reasons for allowing divorce, Jesus directed His disciples back to God's original plan for marriage.

In Matthew 19:9, Jesus mentioned one exception to the permanence of marriage--"except for immorality (*porneia*)." This is usually understood as a reference to marital unfaithfulness. But had Jesus been referring to marital unfaithfulness (adultery), He would have used the Greek word *moicheia*. And we wonder why this "exception clause" was included in Matthew's account, but not Mark's or Luke's record of Jesus teaching on the subject.

Many scholars, including myself, believe that the exception clause in Matthew 5:32 and 19:9 refers to incestuous marriage which was prohibited by Mosaic law (Lev. 18:6-18). Jesus seems to be saying that marriage is permanent, unless you are *illegally* (ie. incestuously) married, as was the case of Herod Antipas who had married his brother's wife (Matt. 14:3-4). In such a case, divorce would be necessitated by biblical law. In all other cases, according to Jesus, the marriage union was divinely intended to be binding for life. The apostle Paul followed the teaching of Jesus, also affirming the permanence of marriage until death (1 Cor. 7:10-11,39). For further discussion on this difficult and controversial subject, please consult my book, *The Divorce Myth* (Bethany House Publishers, 1981).

About Faith

One morning when Jesus was walking from Bethany to Jerusalem, He encountered a fig tree that had lots of leaves, but no fruit. The presence of the leaves indicated that there ought to be fruit. The fig tree had made a false profession. Jesus judged the tree for its false profession saying, "No longer shall there be any fruit from you" (Matt. 21:19). And immediately the fig tree withered.

The disciples were amazed by this miracle and asked, "How did the fig tree wither all at once?" (Matt. 21:20). Jesus' answer provides an important teaching on faith. He said, "Truly I say to you, if you have faith and do not doubt, you will not only do what was done to the fig tree, but even if you say to this mountain, 'be taken up and cast into the sea,' it will happen" (Matt. 21:21). From His vantage point on the Mount of Olives, Jesus may have gazed south to the Herodion fortress which King Herod had built by moving a mountain of dirt to defend the citadel. The result was the most symmetrical and distinguished mountain-fortress in the vicinity of Jerusalem. Looking east from the Herodion to the Rift Valley, the disciples may have wondered, "could believing prayer move that mountain into the Dead Sea?"

The answer is "Yes!" This is confirmed by the words of Jesus, "And all things you ask in prayer, believing you will receive" (Matt. 21:22). The writer of Hebrews defines faith as "the assurance of things hoped for, the conviction of things not seen" (Heb. 11:1). The writer goes on in Hebrews 11 to recount the amazing accomplishments of God's people through faith.

148

About Fasting

Fasting, along with almsgiving and prayer, was one of the three great pillars of Jewish piety in the time of Jesus (Tobit 12:8). And while Jesus never commanded His disciples to fast, He did provide instructions on how fasting was to be done. It must be emphasized that fasting is not the same as dieting. Skipping breakfast or lunch to lose weight may be a good thing, but it is not biblical fasting. Fasting is the act of going without food for the purpose of devoting oneself to God in prayer. Fasting in the Bible is always associated with seeking God through serious and fervent prayer (1 Sam. 7:6; Ezra 8:21; Acts 13:3; 14:23). There was only one fast day prescribed in the Mosaic Law, and that was on the Day of Atonement (Lev. 16:29-34). But other fast days were added in Jewish tradition (Zech. 8:19).

Fasting is a helpful spiritual discipline, but it was not intended as a means of putting on a show. Some Jews in the time of Jesus were fasting for the purpose of making a public display of their spirituality. They would put ashes on their heads, dress in old clothes and neglect their personal hygiene. People would say, "Oh, you look terrible today!" They would respond, "Yes, yes, I am fasting." Their motive was to be seen and honored by others. But Jesus instructed His disciples that fasting should be done with a view to God's approval, not man's praise. He said, "When you fast, anoint your head and wash your face so that your fasting will not be noticed by men, but by your Father who is in secret; and your Father who sees what is done in secret will reward you" (Matt. 6:18).

Fasting makes us weak physically and reminds us of our dependence on God for His sustenance and strength. And that's a good thing. One of the best things about fasting is *breaking* the fast. A meal is never so delicious and satisfying as it is after a period of fasting.

About Family

Jesus had some pretty tough things to say about the family. He warned about a coming day when a man would be set against his father, a daughter against her mother, daughter-in-law against her mother-in-law and a person's enemies would be members of his own household (Matt. 10:35-36). This doesn't appear to be a time for happy families. A careful look at the context indicates that Jesus was speaking of a time when families would be divided because of a family member's allegiance to Israel's Messiah. An unbeliever's hostility against Jesus may someday be so intense that they will express it against family members who love and follow Him. Whew! Discipleship can be very costly.

On another occasion when Jesus was speaking to the crowds, His mother and brothers came seeking to speak with Him (Matt. 12:46-47). When Jesus was told, He raised the question, "Who is My mother and who are My brothers" (Matt. 12:48). He proceeded to answer the question Himself. Stretching out His hand toward His disciples, Jesus said, "Behold My mother and My brothers" (Matt. 12:50). Then He added, "For whoever does the will of My Father who is in heaven, he is My brother and sister and mother." Jesus was saying that spiritual relationships take precedent over family relationships. Our ultimate and eternal family is made up of those who share our faith as followers of Jesus.

It is a hard thing to say, but discipleship may cost some people their family relationships. I know of believers who have been rejected by their families after becoming followers of Jesus. Pressing the point home, Jesus said, "He who loves father or mother more than Me is not worthy of Me; and he who loves son or daughter more than Me is not worthy of Me (Matt. 10:37). Nobody wants to lose family relationships in order to gain Christ. But some people will have to pay that price to be faithful followers of Jesus. Have we counted the cost of following Jesus? Are we ready to pay the price?

About Fear

Children are often afraid of the dark, loud noises and barking dogs. Many people are afraid of death, or worse, the process of dying. Some people are afraid of running out of money during their retirement years. What are you afraid of?

Jesus responded to the fears we have by saying, "Don't be afraid." I counted 15 times in the gospels where Jesus spoke these words of assurance and comfort to His disciples. He pointed to the sparrow saying, "Not one of them will fall to the ground apart from your Father" (Matt. 10:29). If God has such concern for the sparrow, what should His sons and daughters have to fear? So Jesus reminded his disciples, "Do not fear; you are more valuable than many sparrows" (Matt. 10:31). David assured us in Psalm 34:10, "The young lions do lack and suffer hunger; but they who seek the LORD shall not be in want of any good thing." When we experience fear and anxiety, the Apostle Peter reminds us to cast all our concerns on God "because He cares for you" (1 Pet. 5:7).

About Forgiveness

Jesus taught his disciples to forgive others in the same way as they have received God's forgiveness. In His pattern for prayer, Jesus instructed His followers to pray, "And forgive us our debts, as we also have forgiven our debtors" (Matt. 6:12). One day the Apostle Peter asked Jesus, "Lord, how often shall my brother sin against me and I forgive him? Up to seven times?" (Matt. 18:21). Peter assumed that there had to be a limit in forgiving someone who persistently sinned against him. He calculated that *seven* times would be a sufficient expression of grace.

Jesus responded to Peter saying, "I do not say to you, up to seven times, but up to seventy times seven" (Matt. 18:22). Interestingly, the Greek text actually reads "seventy-seven," not "seventy times seven." The only other place where the number "seventy-seven" is found in the Bible is Genesis 4:24 where Lamech boasts, "I have killed a man for wounding me, a young man for injuring me; If Cain is avenged seven times, then Lamech *seventy-seven* times". Boastful Lamech wanted extravagant revenge. Jesus taught that His followers should be Lamech's polar opposite—forgiving repeatedly and extravagantly. According to Jesus, Christian forgiveness knows no limitation. It is a state of the heart, not a matter of mathematical calculation.

Jesus followed up his teaching on forgiveness with a parable (Matt. 18:23-35). Jesus told of a king who was settling accounts with servants who owed him money. One of his servants owed him 10,000 talents—a huge amount. But since he was unable to pay, the king felt compassion on him and graciously forgave the debt. But then the same servant demanded payment of a tiny debt which was owed to him by a fellow servant. Rather than demonstrating the grace which he had received from the king, the wicked servant had the debtor thrown in prison. When the king heard what had happened, he summoned the wicked servant and said, "You wicked slave, I forgave you all the debt because you pleaded with me. Should you not also have had mercy on your fellow slave in the same way that I had mercy on you?" (Matt. 18:32-33).

Jesus' teaching on forgiveness does not remove accountability for our actions or the consequences of sin. A person who is genuinely forgiven may have to suffer the unpleasant consequences of their sin. Criminal behavior may be forgiven, but can still result in a prison sentence.

It is easier to talk about forgiveness than to do it. I recall making a list on my computer of the offenses I had experienced by a Christian brother over a period of years. My list was three pages long! I kept the list for some time while bitterness and resentment seethed in my heart. Then I was prompted by the Holy Spirit to recognize my own sinful attitude. I knew I had to take action. So I printed the list, read it for the final time, struck a match and burned it. Done!

Have you ever thought to yourself, "I could never forgive someone who would do that!" Could the words of Jesus correct that attitude? What Jesus emphasized in

His teaching on forgiveness is that in light of the HUGE pardon we have received, no sin or injustice is too great for disciples to forgive others. Jesus gave us an example of the heart of forgiveness when He prayed for those who had crucified Him, "Father, forgive them, for they do not know what they are doing" (Lk. 23:34).

About the Future

Jesus had quite a bit to say about the future. He told His own disciples about His coming death and resurrection (Matt. 16:21). In His Olivet Discourse, Jesus announced the destruction of the Jerusalem temple (Matt. 24:2), a prophecy which was fulfilled by the Romans in A.D. 70. During His resurrection appearance before Mary, Jesus announced His ascension to heaven (Jn. 20:17). Jesus also told His disciples about the future building of the church (Matt. 16:18), growth of the kingdom (Matt. 13:31-32), persecution of His followers (Jn. 15:18-21, 16:1-4) and His return to heaven to prepare them an eternal home (Jn. 14:2-3).

Jesus had a great deal to say about the "last days" of the present age in his Olivet Discourse (Matt. 24-25). Jesus told of wars, famines and earthquakes leading up to a period of "tribulation" during which His followers would be persecuted and killed (Matt. 24:9). Jesus said that during this period of lawlessness and intense persecution, many false messiahs and false prophets would appear, showing signs and wonders in their attempt to mislead people (Matt. 24:24). At the end of this period, Jesus said that He would return and gather His people from the far reaches of the earth into His kingdom (Matt. 24:27-31).

154

The time of His return is said by Jesus to be a secret, known only by His heavenly Father. (Matt. 24:36).

Jesus announced that after His return to earth with His holy angels, He would assume His promised throne (2 Sam. 7:12-16; Matt. 25:31) and gather the people of the nations for judgment. This judgment will separate Jesus' followers from those who, by their rejection of the King, will be excluded from His eternal kingdom (Matt. 25:32-34,46). Jesus' own followers will enjoy the blessings of eternal life in God's kingdom forever, whereas the unbelieving will be separated from God "into the eternal fire which has been prepared for the devil and his angels" (Matt. 25:41). Much of what Jesus said about the future has been literally fulfilled. These fulfillments give us assurance that Jesus' other predictions about the future will be fulfilled as well.

About Fruit

This past week my wife, Nancy, and I organized three days of "Cousins Camp" for our grandchildren. The spiritual lessons focused on the work of the Holy Spirit in producing fruit in our lives (Gal. 5:22-23). Jesus had a lot to say about fruit and being fruitful.

In his Sermon on the Mount, Jesus taught His disciples that they could know a person's spiritual condition by their fruit. Just as grapes are not gathered from thorn bushes nor figs from thistles, "So every good tree bears good fruit, but the bad tree bears bad fruit. A good tree cannot produce bad fruit, nor can a bad tree produce good fruit" (Matt. 7:16-18). The context of Jesus' teaching on fruit is a warning about false prophets (Matt.

155

7:15). Jesus wanted His disciples to be able to discern the difference between a faithful teacher of God's truth and one who is a "wolf in sheep's clothing." So He warned, "you will know them by their fruit" (Matt. 7:20).

Jesus added to His teaching on fruit during His last Passover with the apostles in the Upper Room. On the night before His crucifixion, Jesus taught an essential lesson on fruit bearing. He said, "Abide in Me, and I in you. As the branch cannot bear fruit of itself unless it abides in the vine, so neither can you unless you abide in Me. I am the vine, you are the branches; he who abides in Me and I in him, he bears much fruit, for apart from Me you can do nothing" (Jn. 15:4-5). The key lesson taught here is that *fruit-bearing results from having a life-giving connection with Jesus, the vine.* If there is no fruit, it means that there is no faith-connection with Jesus. If there is a faith-connection with Jesus, true disciples will bear fruit. Jesus added, "My Father is glorified by this, that you bear much fruit, and so prove to be My disciples" (Jn. 15:8). Followers of Jesus give evidence that they are His disciples by bearing fruit!

Many of Jesus' followers wonder what kind of fruit they should be producing. And is there enough fruit to demonstrate that they are His disciples? If we consider the immediate context of this discussion (Jn. 15:7-11), Jesus seems to identify some of the fruits His followers will produce. He points to such fruit as (1) an active prayer life, (2) glorifying the Father, (3) love for God and others, (4) obedience to Jesus' commandments, (5) a joy-filled life. A young tree does not produce as much fruit as a mature tree, so not all followers of Jesus will produce the same amounts of fruit. But if *fruit-bearing results from*

156

abiding in Jesus (Jn. 15:5), then *all* believers will be producing some fruit. And the stark absence of fruit indicates the absence of faith—and the absence of a life-giving connection with Christ, the Vine, who is the ultimate source of life *and* fruit.

About Giving

Jesus was teaching in the Jerusalem temple opposite the treasury, located in the women's court, where the Jews paid the annual half-shekel temple tax and other offerings. In the treasury there were thirteen wooden offering boxes with bronze, trumpet shaped or funnel-like openings. Two of the offering boxes were designated for the temple tax. The others were devoted to various guilt offerings, tithes, alms for the poor and offerings of the Nazirites and lepers. One of the offering boxes was designated for voluntary contributions. Jesus observed how the rich people were making a show of contributing large sums of money (Mk. 12:41). He also noticed a poor widow who quietly deposited two small copper coins, worth about a penny. Then Jesus gave His disciples an important lesson on giving. He said, "this poor widow put in more than all the contributors to the treasury; for they all put in out of their surplus, but she out of her poverty, put in all she owned, all she had to live on" (Mk. 12:43-44). This was an act of faith, as well as being a huge sacrifice. As she gave "all she had to live on," the woman was trusting God to meet her future needs. Jesus was teaching His disciples that a sacrificial offering made by faith is more pleasing to the Lord than the monetary value of the gift.

We might wonder how Jesus knew the amount that the widow had given. When offerings were deposited in the trumpet shaped funnels of the offering boxes, other people in the treasury could not help but notice the sound of the coins clanging and clattering as they slid down the funnel and into the box. The more coins tossed into the funnels, the louder and more noticeable the clang and clatter of the money dropping into the box. This may be what Jesus was alluding to when he said, "So when you give to the poor, do not *sound a trumpet* before you, as the hypocrites do in the synagogues and in the streets, so that they may be honored by men. Truly, I say to you, they have their reward in full" (Matt. 6:2). When the poor widow dropped her money into the offering box, there was a barely perceptible "clink, clink." In contrast to the rich who gave out of their surplus, the widow gave out of her poverty. Her gift was greater because of the greatness of her sacrifice. Jesus doesn't count the dollars we give. He looks into our heart and our willingness to sacrifice.

About God

What Jesus said about God is pretty profound. Many people embrace the teachings of Jesus, but ignore His amazing claims. Jesus called God "My heavenly Father" (Matt. 15:13; 18:35), "My Father who is in heaven" (Matt. 16:17), and "My Father" (Lk. 22:29; Jn. 5:17; 6:32; 8:54, 10:29; 14:23; 15:1,8). Jesus recognized the Father as God, yet He also identified Himself as God. In referring to God the Father, Jesus said, "I and the Father are one" (Jn. 10:30). He later told the apostles during His last

Passover, "He who has seen Me have seen the Father" (Jn. 14:9).

According to the very words of Jesus, He and the Father are bound together in a spiritual union. He said, "Believe me that I am in the Father and the Father is in Me; otherwise believe because of the works themselves" (Jn. 14:11). Jesus pointed to His miracles as evidence of His spiritual unity with God the Father. Jesus does what the Father does (Jn. 5:19,21) and knows what the Father knows (Jn. 5:20). God the Father has given the responsibility of judgment to His son "so that all will honor the Son even as they honor the Father" (Jn. 5:22-23). There is no doubt that Jesus believed and claimed that He shared divinity with God, His heavenly Father.

Lots of people say they are Christians and "believe" in Jesus. But do they believe what Jesus said about Himself? Do they believe that Jesus is God? If they don't believe what Jesus said about Himself, they are not really *believing* in Jesus.

About Good Works

As a pious and faithful Jew, Jesus did good works. He healed the sick, provided food for the poor and restored sight to the blind. Peter witnessed to the Roman centurion, Cornelius, that Jesus, anointed with the Holy Spirit and power, "went about doing good" (Acts 10:38).

In Luke's version of the Sermon on the Mount, Jesus told His disciples, "Love your enemies, and *do good*, and lend, expecting nothing in return; and your reward will be great" (Lk. 6:35). In His teaching about the resurrection, Jesus differentiated people's destinies based on their

159

works. He said, "An hour is coming, in which all who are in the tombs will hear His voice, and will come forth; those who did the good deeds to a resurrection of life, those who committed the evil deeds to a resurrection of judgment" (Jn. 5:28-29). It is clear from the biblical teaching on salvation that good works don't earn us a place in heaven (Eph. 2:8-10). But good works demonstrate what kind of people we are. It is the pattern of Jesus' followers to do *good*. It is the pattern of the unbelieving world to do *evil*. A judgment that considers our works is, in reality, a judgment based on our *faith*.

Doing good is a lifestyle which is firmly grounded in the teachings of the Hebrew Bible (Psa. 34:14, 37:27) and the teachings of Jesus. The Apostle Paul continues this biblical message in his letter to the Galatians when he writes, "So then, while we have opportunity, let us do good to all people, and especially to those who are of the household of the faith" (Gal. 6:10). The importance of "good deeds" is mentioned six times by Paul in his short letter to Titus (1:16; 27,14; 3:1,8,14). The Boy Scout slogan is, "Do a good turn daily." It's a pretty good slogan for Jesus' followers as well.

About Greatness

I enjoy reading biographies about great men and women who have made their mark in history. But I sometimes wonder what makes these people "great" in the eyes of the world. It is helpful to compare and contrast the world's definition of "greatness" with the teaching of Jesus. One day, His disciples asked Jesus, "Who then is greatest in the kingdom of heaven" (Matt. 18:1). Jesus called a child to himself and answered, "Unless you are converted and become like children, you will not enter the kingdom of heaven. Whoever then humbles himself as this child, he is the greatest in the kingdom of heaven" (Matt. 18:3-4). Jesus was saying that from God's perspective, *humility,* rather than exceptional and illustrious accomplishments, is the mark of true greatness.

Jesus reminded His disciples of this important lesson on the last evening with them before His crucifixion. During the Passover meal, Jesus rose from His place, girded himself with a towel, and began washing the disciples' feet. After washing twelve sets of dirty feet, Jesus explained the significance of the foot washing. He said, "I gave you an example that you also should do as I did for you. Truly, truly, I say to you, a slave is not greater than his master, nor is one who is sent greater than the one who sent him" (Jn. 13:15-16). Jesus was reminding His disciples that true greatness is measured by humble service to others. Those who are great in God's kingdom are those who have humbly and sacrificially served others. How are you serving in God's kingdom work today?

About Heaven

It may be surprising that Jesus actually said very little about heaven. He clearly believed in heaven and frequently refers to His "Father in heaven" (Matt. 5:16, 5:45, 5:48, etc.). He believed that heaven is the dwelling place of God (Matt. 6:9). He also believed that heaven was a place of reward (Matt. 5:12; Lk. 6:23), joy (Lk. 15:7), and eternal treasure (Matt. 6:19-20).

One of the most helpful teachings of Jesus about heaven is found in John 14:2-3 where He explained to His disciples that His Father's house was a place with "many mansions." The word translated "mansions" in the King James version is better rendered "dwelling places" or "apartments." Jesus was returning to heaven to prepare a dwelling place for His followers. Then Jesus offered these words of comfort, "If I go and prepare a place for you, I will come again and receive you to Myself, that where I am, there you may be also" (Jn. 14:3). To be "in heaven" is to dwell forever in the Father's house, enjoying blessed fellowship with Jesus and God's family forever.

About Hell

People don't like to talk about hell or hear about hell. Hell is a rather unpopular subject among Christians today. Some contemporary theologians have decided that hell doesn't actually exist. "How could a good and loving God send someone to hell?" they ask. But Jesus did believe in hell and spoke about it often.

Jesus warned His disciples, "Do not fear those who kill the body but are unable to kill the soul; but rather fear Him who is able to destroy both soul and body in hell" (Matt. 10:28). Again, Jesus warned His followers to break free from anything that would cause spiritual stumbling, leading to "eternal fire." He said, "If your eye causes you to stumble, pluck it out and throw it from you. It is better for you to enter life with one eye, than to have two eyes and be cast into the fiery hell" (Matt. 18:9).

The Greek word translated "hell" in our New Testament is "Gehenna," a reference to the deep, L-shaped valley that bends around the Western Hill in Jerusalem. This was the place where wicked King Ahaz sacrificed to idols and "burned his sons in fire" (2 Chron. 28:3). His son, Manasseh, followed in his father's steps (2 Chron. 33:6). When King Josiah led Judah in a spiritual revival, he defiled *Gehenna*, known today as the Hinnom Valley, turning it into a place to dump and burn refuse. So, when Jesus referred to eternal punishment by fire, He used the vivid image of *Gehenna*, a place "where the worm does not die, and the fire is not quenched" (Mk. 9:47-48). The Apostle John describes this place as "the lake of fire" (Rev. 20:14-15).

Jesus made it clear in his Olivet Discourse that there are just two possible eternal destinies. The wicked will "go away into eternal punishment, but the righteous into eternal life" (Matt. 25:46). Hell is the place God "prepared for the devil and his angels" (Matt. 25:41); but those who choose to follow Satan, rather than following Jesus, will join their master in *Gehenna* (hell) forever. And just for the record, God doesn't *send* anyone to hell. People go to hell because they have rejected the one who came to save them from such a final and fiery future.

About Hypocrisy

If you have been to a theater, you have seen actors who assumed a role that is different than who they are in real life. In the first century Greek dramas, actors wore masks, often changing their mask during the play to assume a different role. These actors were called *hypocrites*, a Greek word which means "play actors." A

163

play actor pretends to be someone he or she is not in real life.

Jesus used the word *hypocrite* to describe people who pretended a spiritual life that was not true to reality. They pretended to be men and women of spiritual piety and prayer, when in fact, they were simply "play actors." In Matthew 23, Jesus rebukes the scribes and Pharisees of His day for being "play actors" (*hypocrites*). Jesus likened them to whitewashed tombs which appear beautiful on the outside, but inside "they are full of dead men's bones" (Matt. 23:27).

The first century scribes and Pharisees were not the only people guilty of *pretending* to be pious, spiritual men and women. One of my greatest challenges as a Bible teacher has been to make sure that I am living what I teach and preach. Jesus' rebuke is relevant for His followers today. We must beware of trying to *appear* righteous, when in reality, we are merely "play actors."

About Jerusalem

Jesus frequently visited Jerusalem, where He ministered, taught in the temple and spent time with His disciples. Jerusalem was the place where God's plan for world redemption was culminated with the death, burial and resurrection of Israel's Messiah. Jesus expressed His deep love for the Holy City, but was disappointed in Jerusalem's rejection of His person as Messiah and king. He lamented, "Jerusalem, Jerusalem, who kills the prophets and stones those who are sent to her! How often I wanted to gather your children together, the way a hen gathers her chicks under her wings, and you were unwilling" (Matt. 23:37). Because of Israel's rejection of the promised Messiah, Jerusalem and the magnificent Second Temple would be destroyed (Matt. 23:38; 24:1-2). This prediction of judgment was fulfilled in A.D. 70 when Titus and his Roman legions destroyed and burned the city of Jerusalem. The Arch of Titus in Rome celebrates the Roman victory and destruction of Jerusalem.

But Jesus did not give up on Jerusalem and her people. Jesus predicted that God's people would have a change of heart. He said, "From now on you will not see Me until you say, 'Blessed is He who comes in the name of the Lord'" (Matt. 23:29; Psa. 118:26). God's repentant people await Jesus' return (Zech. 12:10; 13:1; 14:4) when He will reign as king over all the earth from Jerusalem (Zech. 14:9,17).

About Judgment

In Jesus' discussion with Nicodemus about the necessity of new birth as a condition for entering God's kingdom, it was made clear that the purpose of His coming to earth was not to judge people, but to save them. "For God did not send the Son into the world to judge the world, but that the world might be saved through Him" (Jn. 3:17). Jesus didn't enter into humanity for the *purpose* of condemnatory judgment. Yet, there will be judgment based on one's response to the illuminating light of Jesus. Those who respond to the light of Jesus experience His salvation. Those who reject the light of Jesus are left under divine judgment on sin (Jn. 3:18).

Jesus had more to say about judgment after healing the lame man at the Pool of Bethesda. Responding to the questions raised by the Jewish leaders about His Sabbath healing, Jesus pointed out that He does the works of the Father and shares equally in God's divine authority (Jn. 5:19-21). This authority includes judgment. Jesus said, "For not even the Father judges anyone, but He has given all judgment to the Son, so that all will honor the Son even as they honor the Father." (Jn. 5:22-23). Jesus did not come to earth for the purpose of judging sinners. But just as light can be thwarted and cast a shadow of darkness, so rejection of God's only provision of deliverance leaves sinners under judgment. Jesus is the ultimate and final judge (Matt. 25:31-46; Rev. 20:10-15).

Jesus taught that there are degrees of judgment depending on the opportunity one has been given to respond to God's message of salvation. Jesus denounced the cities of Chorazin, Bethsaida and Capernaum where He did most of his great miracles (Matt. 11:20-23). But in spite of the revelation they had received, the people of these cities refused to repent. Jesus announced, "It will be more tolerable for the land of Sodom in the day of judgment, than for you" (Matt. 11:22). Jesus taught that the greater the light received, the greater the accountability and consequent judgment on the sin of unbelief.

It has been a great privilege and blessing to study and teach the Bible, as I have during my forty-year career as a seminary professor. But I also know that there is increased accountability that accompanies this sacred stewardship. I am often reminded the sobering words of James, the Lord's half-brother, who wrote that teachers "will incur a stricter judgment" (Jms. 3:1).

About the Kingdom

Jesus began His public ministry by announcing, "Repent, for the Kingdom of Heaven is at hand" (Matt. 4:17). Interestingly, it was not a new message. In fact, it was the same message that His forerunner, John the Baptizer, had proclaimed (Matt. 3:2). Jesus spent His three-and-a-half-year ministry teaching and preaching about God's kingdom. Many of His parables were designed to teach His disciples about the kingdom. In Matthew 13 Jesus repeatedly declared, "The kingdom of heaven is like...."

It is crucial to understand that the "kingdom of God" or "kingdom of heaven" is not a new theme with either John or Jesus. From the time that God's sovereign rule over the earth was first challenged by Satan (Gen. 3), God has been working to reassert His rule over His creation. God's kingdom was foreshadowed in the person of King David, to whom it was promised that he would have a son who would sit on his throne and rule and reign forever (2 Sam. 7:16). The angel Gabriel announced to Mary that God's kingdom program would be fulfilled by Jesus, Israel's messianic king (Lk. 1:32-33).

God's kingdom program involves a *king* who rules, a *people* who are ruled, and a *place* where this rule is recognized. We may define the kingdom of God (or kingdom of heaven) as "God's people in God's place under God's rule." Some teach that God's kingdom is a *present* reality as Jesus rules from His throne in heaven. Others teach that God's kingdom is a *future* reality that will begin when Jesus returns to judge the nations and assume David's earthly throne in Jerusalem.

From the teachings of Jesus and other New Testament writings, I have concluded that the kingdom of God is a present, spiritual reality which will be consummated in physical form at the Second Coming of Jesus. As some theologians have expressed it, the kingdom of God is "already, but not yet." The kingdom of God is *already* inaugurated by the coming of the King, but *not yet* consummated as it will be when the King Jesus returns.

Jesus said that His kingdom is like a mustard seed that starts small, but grows to great proportions (Matt. 13:31-32). Again, Jesus likened His kingdom to the leavening process where a little bit of leaven permeates the whole loaf (Matt. 13:33). He explained that the present form of the kingdom would include weeds ("tares") which will be gathered and burned at the end of this present age (Matt. 13:36-43). Jesus used the parable of the hidden treasure and great pearl to illustrate the preeminent value of God's kingdom (Matt. 13:44-46). Using the parable of the dragnet, Jesus explained how God would separate the righteous from the wicked (Matt. 13:47-50) in preparation for the future culmination of His kingdom. Many of Jesus' miracles serve to reveal the blessings of coming under the rule of the King. These blessings include peace, plenty, justice, healing, physical safety and security (Isa. 2:4, 11:6-9, 35:5-6). Accepting the rule of King Jesus means entering His kingdom (Col. 1:13). The full measure of the promised kingdom blessings must await His return.

About the Law

The word "law" (Greek *nomos*) is the New Testament translation of the Hebrew word, *torah*, comes from a verb (*yarah*) which means "to teach." The noun form (*torah*) simply means "teaching" or "instruction." *Torah* can refer to the teaching a father gives his son or the instruction God gave Israel. The *torah* or "law" given to Israel was simply the Lord's instruction.

Jesus was a law-abiding Jew. Never in any of His teaching did Jesus undermine or invalidate the instruction that God gave His people Israel at Mount Sinai. In His Sermon on the Mount, Jesus said, "Do not think that I came to abolish the Law or the Prophets; I did not come to abolish but to fulfill. For truly I say to you, until heaven and earth pass away, not the smallest letter or stroke shall pass from the Law until all is accomplished" (Matt. 5:17-18).

Although Jesus established a New Covenant through His sacrificial death for the redemption of sinners (Lk. 22:20, Heb. 8:6-13), He didn't change or annul God's instruction ("law"). His teaching in the Sermon on the Mount ("you have that it was said, ... but I say to you") did not modify the law, but simply directed His Jewish listeners back to the original intent of the law which focused on the heart attitude, not merely the superficial performance of God's commandments.

A good example of Jesus' adherence to the law is the case of the woman caught in the act of adultery (Jn. 8:2-11). The religious leaders were testing Jesus to see if He would keep the law which required the death penalty for adultery (Lev. 20:10, Deut. 22:22-27). Jesus responded,

169

"He who is without sin among you, let him be the first to throw a stone at her" (Jn. 8:7). Jesus agreed that the adulteress should be stoned, but only if there were qualified witnesses. Deuteronomy 19:15-21 required that the witnesses in a court case be non-malicious in their testimony. The words "without sin" in the judicial context of John 8:1-11 mean "competent to testify." Jesus, a law abiding-Jew, was saying in effect, "If there are competent witnesses with non-malicious intent, let the stoning begin!" The religious leaders had set up the woman for the purpose of accusing Jesus (Jn. 8:6). The trial ended without a verdict and the woman's accusers made a quick exit. Jesus was better at adhering to the requirements of the law than the scribes and Pharisees who initiated the court case! It was not because of "grace" that the woman was not condemned by Jesus; but because the witnesses, who were guilty of the malicious intent, were not competent to testify by Mosaic Law. The legal case against the adulterous woman collapsed. The fact that Jesus didn't approve her sin is evidenced by His words, "Go. From now on sin no more" (Jn. 8:11).

About Love

There are three different Greek words used in the New Testament that can be translated "love." There was a word for brotherly love (*philos*) and another for family love (*storge*). But the word that Jesus used most frequently was *agape*. This word refers to a sacrificial love that does what is in the best interest of others, even at great personal cost. The noun form of this word (*agapao*) is used in John 3:16, "For God so loved the world, that He gave His only begotten Son, ..." Jesus exhibited this "sacrificial love" by submitting to the Father's will in giving His life for the sins of fallen humanity.

During His last Passover meal with His disciples in the Upper Room, Jesus introduced a "new commandment." He said, "A new commandment I give to you, that you love (*agapao*) one another, even as I have loved (*agapao*) you, that you also love one another. By this all people will know that you are my disciples if you have love (*agape*) for one another" (Jn. 13:34-35). Agape love is the timeless identification badge of Jesus' followers. Are you wearing that identifying mark?

Jesus used the word "love" again when a Jewish lawyer asked his opinion as to "the great commandment" in the law (Matt. 22:36). Jesus answered by quoting Deuteronomy 6:5, "You shall *love* (*agapao*) the Lord your God with all your heart, and with all your soul, and with all your mind." But He went a step further by identifying the commandment of Leviticus 19:18 as second only to the first, "You shall love (*agapao*) your neighbor as yourself." Jesus lived and taught God's great law of *agape* love.

About Marriage

Jesus was questioned by some Pharisees, "Is it lawful for a man to divorce his wife for any reason at all?" In His reply, Jesus appealed to God's original plan for marriage in Genesis 2:24, "For this reason a man shall leave his father and mother and be joined to his wife, and the two shall become one flesh." Jesus concluded His response by giving a strong affirmation of the permanence of the marriage union, "What therefore God has joined together, let no man separate" (Matt. 19:6). This was the final answer to the Pharisees' question, "Is it lawful for a man to divorce his wife?" Jesus' answer is clearly, "No!"

It was later that day that Jesus' disciples questioned Him further on the subject of marriage (Mk.10:10). Jesus added this comment, "Whoever divorces his wife and marries another woman commits adultery against her; and if she herself divorces her husband and marries another man, she is committing adultery" (Mk. 10:11-12).

Jesus' disciples apparently took a more lenient view on marriage than He did and responded by saying, "If the relationship of a man with his wife is like this, it is better not to marry" (Matt. 19:10). In other words, "If you can't get out of your marriage, maybe it is better not to get married!" Jesus offered His disciples three reasons why someone might not marry. Jesus said, "There are eunuchs who were born that way from their mother's womb; and there are eunuchs who are made eunuchs by men; and there are also eunuchs who made themselves eunuchs for the sake of the kingdom of heaven" (Matt. 19:12). A "eunuch" was a man whose male organ had been removed so he could serve the king's harem without the risk of sexual temptation. Jesus used the term "eunuch" as a metaphor for someone who does not marry.

The *first* reason why someone may not marry is due to birth. A congenital defect of some sort prevents the possibility of marriage. The *second* reason appears to be a reference to someone who, because of life's circumstances, is unable to marry. This may have been due to a neutering procedure or simply never being asked to marry. The *third* reason someone may not marry is due to a personal decision motivated by kingdom priorities.

The early Christians understood that this third reason for not marrying was because of a previous divorce and a desire to honor Jesus' teaching about the permanence of marriage.

Both Jesus and the Apostle Paul held to a high view of marriage and taught that the marriage union was intended by God's design to be permanent until death (Matt.19:6; 1 Cor. 7:39; Rom. 7:2-3). It is clear that death dissolves the marriage union and that the institution of marriage is not continued into eternity (Matt. 22:30).

Many people have struggled to maintain their marriages, but have failed. Some have chosen to remarry. Others are committed to remaining single with a view to restoring the broken relationship. Whatever situation you find yourself in, we can be assured of God's love and forgiveness for our past failures. Remember, God is always willing to forgive, restore and bless those who acknowledge their sin and repent.

About the Messiah

"Messiah" (Hebrew *mashiach*) is actually a Hebrew word and means "anointed one." A *messiah* in the Hebrew Bible was one who had been anointed with oil in a sacred ceremony which set the person apart as God's representative. The term "messiah" was the appropriate term to describe God's anointed king, priest, prophet or individual God had appointed for a special purpose. The term is even used of King Cyrus whom God had raised up to defeat Babylon and decree the return of the Judeans at the end of their seventy-year exile (Isa. 45:1).

The term "Christ" (*christos*) is the Greek equivalent of the Hebrew word *messiah (mashiach).* "Christ," as it appears in the New Testament, is not a proper name but a designation added to the name of Jesus to identify Him as Israel's promised Messiah.

Jesus did not discuss the concept of Israel's Messiah, nor did He call Himself "Messiah" (or "Christ"). But three times in the Gospels He accepted the designation (Matt. 16:16-17; Mk. 14:61-62; Jn. 4:26). There is no doubt that the disciples believed that Jesus was Israel's promised Messiah (Matt. 16:16).

Even Jesus' enemies recognized, but denied, His messianic claims. During His trial, Jesus was told by Israel's high priest, "tell us whether you are the Christ, the Son of God" (Matt. 27:63). Jesus answered by identifying Himself with the messianic "Son of Man" whose coming was prophesied by Daniel (Dan. 7:13). The high priest tore his robes and declared, "He has blasphemed (Matt. 27:65). Instead of recognizing Jesus as their Messiah, the Jewish leaders concluded, "He deserves death." In spite of Jesus' message and miracles, Israel's Messiah was rejected and crucified. As John commented in the prologue of his gospel, "He came to His own, and those who were His own did not receive Him" (Jn. 1:11).

About Miracles

The gospels record about 35 specifically detailed miracles that Jesus performed during His earthly ministry. Many other miracles are referred to more generally. These miracles served to authenticate Jesus as Israel's divine Messiah (Jn. 20:30-31) and the offer of His kingdom message for the people of Israel (Matt. 4:23, 9:35). The Apostle John calls Jesus' miracles "signs" (*semeion*) because they point the way to Jesus. The word that Jesus used most frequently to refer to His miracles is the word "works" (*ergon*). The miracles are simply Jesus' works. He said, "If I do not do the works (*ergon*) of My Father, do not believe Me; but if I do them, though you do not believe Me, believe the works (*ergon*), so that you may know and understand that the Father is in Me, and I in the Father" (Jn. 10:37-38).

Jesus denounced the cities of Chorazin, Bethsaida and Capernaum because the people had witnessed so many of his miracles, but they didn't receive the message. They didn't welcome and believe in the one to whom the "signs" pointed. Jesus announced that there would be greater judgment on these cities than on wicked Sodom "because they did not repent" (Matt. 11:20).

One day when the religious leaders asked Jesus for another "sign," He rebuked them for rejecting the miracles which had already been given. Jesus announced that there would be no further signs to unbelieving Israel except for "the sign of Jonah the prophet" (Matt. 12:39). Jesus further explained that as Jonah was three days and three nights in the belly of the great fish, so Jesus would undergo an astonishingly similar experience (Matt. 12:40). The comparison with Jonah highlights the similar time period and the surprise ending. As Jonah was delivered from the great fish, so Jesus was resurrected from the grave. Jesus pointed to His resurrection as the ultimate and final miracle or sign authenticating His deity and messiahship to the people of Israel. Are you looking for a sign that Jesus is whom He claimed to be—God's Son and Israel's Messiah? Look no further than the miracle of His resurrection!

About Money

All of us need money to buy food, pay rent and purchase the things required to maintain ourselves and our families here on planet earth. While we all need money, Jesus warned against making it the focus of our lives. Instead of making earthly treasure our ultimate pursuit, Jesus said, "Store up for yourselves treasures in heaven, where neither moth nor rust destroys, and where thieves do not break in or steal; for where your treasure is, your heart will be also" (Matt. 6:20-21). Then He added that "No one can serve two masters; for either he will hate the one and love the other, or he will be devoted to one and despise the other. You cannot serve God and wealth" (Matt. 6:24). Jesus was saying that both God and money are masters. And followers of Jesus must decide which they will serve.

Excessive concern for money is often the result of worry. How will my family survive since I lost my job? What am I to do about these unpaid bills? Will I have enough money to live on when I retire? Instead of worrying about these physical needs, Jesus told His disciples, "But seek first His kingdom and His righteousness, and all these things will be added to you" (Matt. 6:33). David experienced God's provision when he was an outcast from the royal court of Saul, fleeing for his life in the Judean wilderness. It was in that context of need that he acknowledged, "The young lions do lack and suffer hunger; but they who seek the LORD shall not be in want of any good thing" (Ps. 34:10).

Money is morally neutral. It is neither good nor bad. It is our *attitude* toward money that concerned Jesus. Is money a useful tool or an seductive idol? Are we hoarders or stewards of the resources entrusted to us? There is nothing wrong with having money. As Paul points out, it is "the *love* of money" that leads to all sorts of evil and undermines our faith (1 Tim. 6:10).

Many believers have found that the practice of giving money away serves as a helpful deterrent against being overly focused on money. Open-handed generosity toward others--our church, local charities, Christian organizations and missions--helps keep our focus on using our money in ways that count for eternity. All the money we possess will be left behind when we die. The only way to "keep it," is using it to "store up treasures in heaven" (Matt. 6:20), making investments in God's kingdom.

About Neighbors

One day a Jewish lawyer asked Jesus, "Which is the great commandment in the law?" Jesus answered by quoting Deuteronomy 6:5 to show that loving God is the great and foremost commandment. Then He added, "The second is like it, 'You shall love your neighbor as yourself'" (Matt. 22:39). Seeking to justify himself, the lawyer probed further, "And who is my neighbor?" (Lk. 10:29).

Jesus told the familiar story of the Good Samaritan (Lk. 10:30-37) in answer to the lawyer's question, "Who is

177

my neighbor?" A man was traveling on a road through the Judean wilderness from Jerusalem to Jericho. Along the way he was robbed, beaten and left half dead. By chance a priest was traveling down the same road, but passed on the other side. Later a Levite came by, but he too quickly passed. Surprisingly, it was a despised Samaritan (see John 4:9) who "felt compassion" on the unfortunate traveler. He not only bandaged his wounds, but took him to an innkeeper whom the good Samaritan paid to care for the man he had rescued.

Jesus concluded the story and asked the lawyer, "Which of these three do you think proved to be a neighbor to the man who fell into the robbers' hands" (Lk. 10:36). The answer was obvious. The "neighbor" was the Samaritan who showed mercy on the robbed and injured man. Jesus concluded the encounter with the lawyer saying, "Go and do the same" (Lk. 10:37).

The lawyer's question, "who is my neighbor?" is relevant today. Jesus' parable teaches us that my neighbor is (1) someone who has a need, (2) I know about the need, and (3) I have the resources to meet that need. I have sometimes passed by opportunities to be a good neighbor because I was in a hurry and had a schedule to keep. Then later, I looked back with regret for missing a chance to be a blessing to someone in need. May the Lord help us to be alert to future opportunities to follow the Samaritan's example as a good neighbor.

About Oaths

An oath is like a promise, but even more serious. It is a solemn pledge or vow often used to express someone's commitment to a course of action. When a young man or woman joins the United States military, they take the following oath: "I, (*your name*), do solemnly swear that I will support and defend the Constitution of the United States against all enemies, foreign and domestic; that I will bear true faith and allegiance to the same; and that I will obey the orders of the President of the United States and the orders of the officers appointed over me, according to regulations and the Uniform Code of Military Justice. So help me God." My dad made this pledge when he joined the United States Navy. My son raised his right hand and repeated this oath when he entered the United States Naval Academy.

In His Sermon on the Mount, Jesus spoke about the seriousness of making an oath. He condemned false oaths and vows that were made without wholehearted commitment. Better than making superficial or halfhearted vows, Jesus said, "Make no oath at all, either by heaven, for it is the throne of God; or by earth, for it is the footstool of His feet; or by Jerusalem, for it is the city of the Great King" (Matt. 5:34-35). Instead of having to back up every statement with an oath, Jesus directed His followers to simply speak the truth always. He said, "Let your statement be, 'Yes, yes' or 'No, no'; anything beyond these is of evil" (Matt. 5:36; also Jms. 5:12).

Jesus didn't condemn all oaths; but, in keeping with God's law (Lev. 19:12), He denounced the hypocrisy of false and flippant oaths. God Himself made an oath when He appointed Jesus as high priest forever (Psa. 110:4, Heb. 7:20-21). God keeps His promises and wants His people to be promise keepers too (Ecc. 5:4).

About Peace

Peace treaties and promises of peace are so often broken. The hopes and expectations of those who are searching and hoping for the end of conflict are not realized or fulfilled. Yet, Jesus promised peace. He said, "Peace I leave with you; My peace I give to you; not as the world gives do I give to you. Do not let your heart be troubled, nor let it be fearful" (Jn. 14:26). Jesus promised to give *His* peace to His followers! This is not a peace based on the changing circumstances of world conditions. The peace that Jesus promised is based on an unchanging relationship with God through His Son, Israel's Messiah.

The peace that is available through Jesus is not merely the absence of conflict, but includes the positive benefits of His work of redemption. Because of our sin, we were once alienated from God and subject to His wrathful judgment. But on the basis of Jesus' sacrifice, believers are reconciled with God (2 Cor. 5:18) and are at peace with their Creator. Paul sums up this work of reconciliation in Romans 5:1 where he writes, "Therefore, having been justified by faith, we have *peace with God* through our Lord Jesus Christ."

About Persecution

Being a follower of Jesus is not an easy path to walk. Early in His earthly ministry, Jesus began telling His disciples that they would be "persecuted for the sake of righteousness" (Matt. 5:10). In His Olivet Discourse, Jesus told His followers that persecution would increase in the last days. He said, "Then they will deliver you to tribulation, and will kill you, and you will be hated by all nations because of my name" (Matt. 24:9). Writing from Rome toward the end of his ministry, Paul informed Timothy, "All who desire to live godly in Christ Jesus will be persecuted" (2 Tim. 3:12).

We wonder why Christians experience such hatred and hostility from the unbelieving world. Jesus answered that question for His disciples during His last Passover in the Upper Room. He gave three reasons for the world's hatred and persecution of believers. *First*, The world hates the believers because of the essential difference in nature between the world and the disciples. The world loves its own--those who belong to it. But it hates those who have been delivered from the world by Jesus (Jn. 15:19). *Second*, the world hates the believers because of their identification with the rejected Christ. Since the world persecuted Jesus, it will persecute His followers (Jn. 15:20). *Third*, the world hates the followers of Jesus because they don't know God, the Father (Jn. 15:21).

In his book, *The Global War on Christians*, John L. Allen writes, "Christians today indisputably are the most persecuted religious body on the planet." This is not simply one writer's opinion. Allen demonstrates through careful documentation that this is an undeniable fact. As the values and opinions of society move dramatically to the left, Christians are finding themselves on the isolated and rejected fringe of American culture rather than in the mainstream. If what Jesus said was true, we should not expect the unbelieving world's attitude toward Christians to change anytime soon. Followers of Jesus must live with the expectation of increasing persecution and prepare themselves spiritually to endure it. Jesus revealed this beforehand so that we won't be taken by surprise when persecution comes our way (Jn. 16:1-4).

About the Pharisees

Contrary to popular opinion, the Pharisees were not the worst people alive in the time of Jesus. In fact, they were a lot like evangelical Christians today. They loved God. They loved His Word. They believed the Bible and embraced its great doctrines, like the resurrection. They were middle class folks who held to the traditions they had been taught in the synagogue. Josephus describes the Pharisees as "excelling the rest of their nation in the observances of religion, and as exact exponents of the laws" (*Jewish War* 1.110). In addition to being "the most accurate interpreters of the laws," Josephus comments that the Pharisees "are affectionate to each other and cultivate harmonious relations with the community" (*Jewish War* 2.162, 166). The Pharisees were what you would call "good people." But like many Christians today, they had a problem.

Jesus revealed this problem when He spoke to the crowds regarding the scribes and Pharisees. Jesus said, "All that they tell you, do and observe, but do not do according to their deeds; for they say things and do not do them" (Matt. 23:2-3). The problem with the Pharisees, and with many followers of Jesus today, is hypocrisy. The Greek word translated "hypocrite" (*hupokrites*) was used in ancient times of the actors who played various parts in the Greek theater. The actors would often play several different roles in the drama, putting on different masks to change their voice and appearance. These "play actors" pretended to be someone different than who they actually were.

In Matthew 23, Jesus condemns the scribes and Pharisees as "hypocrites," play actors who were performing the outward act of being devoted to God; but this was not their true identity. Like the actors in a Greek drama, they were pretending to be someone they were not. Jesus pronounced seven "woes" on these religious leaders who had mastered the art of parading their pretended piety. "Woe to you, scribes and Pharisees, hypocrites! For you are like whitewashed tombs which on the outside appear beautiful, but inside they are full of dead men's bones and all uncleanness" (Matt. 23:27).

One of the greatest temptations Christians face is pretending to have spiritual life and vitality that isn't really there. May it not be said of us, that we are play actors merely *pretending* to be sincere followers of Jesus while our true affections are elsewhere.

About the Poor

Jesus was concerned about the poor. In fact, He blessed them saying, "Blessed are you who are poor, for yours is the kingdom of God" (Lk. 6:20). During a visit in Nazareth at His hometown synagogue, Jesus read from the text of Isaiah 61:1, "The Spirit of the Lord is upon Me, because He has anointed Me to preach the gospel to the poor" (Lk. 4:18). Jesus told a godly man who was seeking eternal life to sell his possessions and give the proceeds to the poor (Mk. 10:21). Jesus honored the poor widow who gave sacrificially out of her poverty in contrast to others who gave out of their abundance (Mk. 12:41-44). The parable of the rich man and poor Lazarus (Lk. 16:19-31) contrasts their two destinies, highlighting the fact that the poor believers of this age will have a glorious future in heaven.

The disciples must have captured their teacher's concern for the poor and suggested that the expensive perfume being used to anoint Jesus at the home of Simon should have been sold and the money "given to the poor" (Matt. 26:6-9). But Jesus corrected them saying, "Why do you bother the woman? For she has done a good deed to Me. For you always have the poor with you; but you do not always have Me" (Matt. 26:10-11). Sacrificial worship of Jesus and generosity toward the poor are not mutually exclusive commitments. It takes wisdom from God to know how to best accomplish *each* of these worthy deeds.

I have struggled over the years to know how to respond to the needs of the poor. Should I give a dollar to every homeless person holding up a sign, "Anything helps!" I fear that my dollar will go toward drugs, cigarettes or alcohol. While food or money may be the appropriate response in some circumstances, I believe that giving to an institution or ministry, like the Portland Rescue Mission, is the most responsible way to help the poor and homeless people in our midst.

About Prayer

Prayer may be simply defined as "talking to God." And Jesus had much to say about this subject. He taught His disciples "the Lord's Prayer" (Matt. 6:9-13; Lk. 11:2-4) to provide them with a *pattern* for prayer. The first priority in the Lord's Prayer is God's concerns; the advancement of His kingdom and the accomplishment His will. The second area of focus is our personal needs; food, forgiveness and deliverance from temptation.

Some people talk about the "power of prayer." It is better to talk about the "power of God" which believers can access through believing prayer. Jesus said, "And all things you ask in prayer, believing, you will receive" (Matt. 21:22).

In His final instructions on prayer during the Passover meal in the Upper Room, Jesus taught His disciples an important key to answered prayer. Disciples are to pray to the Father in the name of Jesus. Jesus said, "Truly, truly, I say to you, if you ask the Father for anything in My name, He will give it to you" (Jn. 16:23).

Concluding our prayers "in Jesus name" is not just a magic formula or a way to "sign off" at the end of a prayer. To pray "in Jesus' name" is to appeal to God the Father on the basis of the merits of his Son. It is like saying to our heavenly Father, "I believe this prayer is consistent with what Jesus wants for me and so I'm signing His name to my request." We can be assured that God will answer prayers asked in Jesus' name "that the Father may be glorified in the Son" (Jn. 14:13).

About Repentance

Jesus began His public ministry preaching, "Repent, for the kingdom of heaven is at hand" (Matt. 4:17). The Greek verb "repent" (*metanoeo*) literally means "change your thinking" and implies a change of direction. People who "repent" stop what they are doing, turn around, and go in the opposite direction. The classic example of repentance is the response of the Thessalonians as witnessed by the Apostle Paul. He recounts how they "turned to God from idols to serve a living and true God" (1 Thess. 1:9). The Thessalonians didn't just stop worshiping idols. They turned away from their idols to serve the true God!

According to Jesus, repentance is closely associated with belief. Those who repent "change their minds," moving from an attitude of unbelief to an attitude of belief. Jesus pointed out that many of those who heard John the Baptizer "did not even feel remorse afterward [i.e. *repent*] so as to believe him [John]" (Matt. 21:32).

John the baptizer insisted that genuine repentance would lead to a changed life. He told the religious leaders who had come to him for baptism, "Bear fruit in keeping with repentance" (Matt. 3:8). Jesus agreed with the requirement of fruit as an evidence of genuine repentance. True believers, He said, will be known "by their fruits" (Matt. 7:20). Then Jesus added this warning, "Not everyone who says to Me, 'Lord, Lord,' will enter the kingdom of heaven, but he who does the will of My Father who is in heaven will enter" (Matt. 7:21).

When Jesus was questioned by the grumbling Pharisees and scribes as to why He would eat and drink with tax gatherers and sinners, He responded, "It is not those who are well who need a physician, but those who are sick. I have not come to call the righteous, but sinners to repentance" (Lk. 5:31-32).

Sinners repent when they change their minds about Jesus, turning from their sinful ways and placing their faith in His redemptive work as Messiah and Savior. This supernatural work is prompted by the Holy Spirit and results in a supernaturally changed life. The invitation to repent stands open and is open to all (Acts 3:19, 11:18).

About Rewards

Although salvation is a gift of God and can't be earned through our good works or sacrifices, Jesus did promise rewards for faithful service in His kingdom. I have never served God to earn a reward, but it is reassuring to know that God recognizes and appreciates our labors for His kingdom. Jesus promised rewards for those who seek God through prayer and fasting for the purpose of honoring Him rather than as a public display of their spiritual piety (Matt. 6:5,16). He also promised reward for those who bear up and endure the world's scorn and insults for identifying themselves as followers of Jesus. He said, "Be glad in that day and leap for joy, for behold your reward is great in heaven (Lk. 6:23).

How should believers respond to the hatred and hostility of their enemies? Jesus commanded His disciples, "Love your enemies, do good, and lend expecting nothing in return; and your reward will be great, ..." (Lk. 6:35). Of course this is easier to say than to do! But as Jesus said, "With God, all things are possible" (Matt. 19:26).

Generous giving as an act of worship will also be rewarded. Jesus said, "Give and it will be given to you. They will pour into your lap a good measure—pressed down, shaken together, and running over. For by your standard of measure it will be measured to you in return" (Lk. 6:38). The reward for open-handed generosity toward your church or those in need is not a promise of financial prosperity. The greatest reward in giving is the joy of sharing in the ministry of people who are serving Jesus! This reward is not measured by dollars, but by the blessing and privilege of partnering with others in doing God's kingdom work.

About Resurrection

The subject of the resurrection was a hotly debated theological controversy among Jews in the first century. The Pharisees embraced the doctrine based on the teaching of the prophets (Ezek. 37:11-14; Dan. 12:2), but the Sadducees rejected this biblical truth. They rejected the resurrection, not because they were liberal, but because they were so conservative! They said, "If Moses didn't teach it, we won't believe it." And since they couldn't find the doctrine of the resurrection in the Torah, they believed that "the soul perishes with the body" (Josephus, *Antiquities* 18.16).

One day the Sadducees challenged Jesus about His belief in the resurrection. They told a story about seven brothers who had been married to the same woman (Matt. 22:23-28). The first died and his brother married the widow. The second brother died and the third brother married the widow and so on until all seven brothers and the widow died. Then, with a bit of a snicker, they asked Jesus, "In the resurrection whose wife of the seven will she be, since all had married her?"

Jesus responded to the challenge by quoting God's own words from Exodus 3:6 in the Torah, the section of the Bible which the Sadducees regarded as authoritative.

Jesus said, "Regarding the resurrection of the dead, have you not read what was spoken to you by God: 'I am the God of Abraham, and the God of Isaac, and the God of Jacob'? He is not the God of the dead but of the living" (Matt. 22:31-32).

Jesus not only believed in the resurrection, He claimed the authority to resurrect the dead (Jn. 5:27-29). Jesus demonstrated this authority when He raised Lazarus from the dead (Jn. 11:17-44). According to the teaching of Jesus, all humanity will participate in a future resurrection of the dead. Believers will participate in "a resurrection of life," while those who have demonstrated their unbelief by their evil deeds will participate in "a resurrection of judgment" (Jn. 5:29; Matt. 25:46). The biblical doctrine of the resurrection is an essential element of the Christian faith. Paul emphasized this in his letter to the Corinthians, "If there is no resurrection of the dead, not even Christ has been raised" (1 Cor. 15:13).

About the Sabbath

The Sabbath was the sign of God's covenant with His people Israel (Exod. 31:13-17). In addition, the Sabbath recalled and commemorated God's rest after the six days of creation and Israel's freedom after 400 years of bondage in Egypt (Exod. 20:8-11; Deut. 5:12-15). As a law abiding Jew, Jesus faithfully kept the Sabbath. However, Jesus didn't always keep the "traditions of the elders" (Mk. 7:3), which the Jewish leaders had added to the Sabbath law to prevent Sabbath violations. In Jewish tradition, there were 39 classes of work which were forbidden on the Sabbath (M. *Shabbat* 7.2). Unless a life was in danger, certain medical remedies were also forbidden on the Sabbath according to the traditions of the elders (M. *Shabbat* 13.4. 21.6). Even lighting a lamp was considered a violation of Sabbath tradition (M. *Shabbat* 2.6). By the time of Jesus, the Sabbath had become a burden rather than the blessing God had intended when He gave Israel the gift of a weekly day of rest.

Jesus' ministry on the Sabbath often led to conflict with the Jewish religious leaders who were trying to enforce the traditions which they had added to the Sabbath law. When Jesus healed the lame man at the Pool of Bethesda on the Sabbath (Jn. 5:1-9), the Jewish leaders began persecuting Him because "He was doing these things on the Sabbath" (Jn. 5:16). After Jesus miraculously gave sight to the man born blind, the Jewish leaders concluded, "we know that this man is a sinner" (Jn. 9:24) since the healing had taken place on the Sabbath.

One day Jesus was walking through the grain fields on the Sabbath. His disciples became hungry and began plucking and eating some heads of grain. When the Pharisees saw this, they pointed out to Jesus, "Look, your disciples do what is not lawful to do on a Sabbath" (Matt. 12:2). Defending His disciples, Jesus reminded the religious leaders of two stories in the Hebrew Bible where requirements of the ceremonial law were subordinated to human needs. Quoting from Hosea 6:6, Jesus rebuked His disciples' accusers saying, "If you had known what it means, 'I desire compassion, and not sacrifice,' you would not have condemned the innocent.'" Concluding His defense of the disciples' actions, Jesus added, "For the Son of Man is Lord of the Sabbath" (Matt. 12:8).

Jesus was saying that the Sabbath was a gift pointing to Jesus who gives His people rest, freedom and blessing. The Sabbath was instituted as a gift for humanity (Mk. 2:27) and was never intended to become a burden through legalistic restrictions and regulations.

About Sacrifice

No one who has become a genuine follower of Jesus has done it without sacrifice. There is a cost of discipleship. John the Baptizer paid for it with his life. James, the half-brother of Jesus, paid for it with his head! Peter and Paul were imprisoned and martyred for following Jesus. This shouldn't surprise us. Jesus said, "He who does not take his cross and follow after Me is not worthy of Me. He who has found his life will lose it, and he who has lost his life for My sake will find it" (Matt. 10:38-39). Dietrich Bonhoeffer, a German pastor who was hanged by the Nazis for opposing Hitler, summed it up well in his book, *The Cost of Discipleship*, when he wrote, "When Christ calls a man, He bids him come and die."

The Christian life is not "easy beliefism." The path of discipleship requires counting the cost and total surrender of our lives. While the cost is real, so are the rewards. As missionary Jim Elliot, who was martyred bringing the gospel to the Auca natives of Ecuador, put it so eloquently, "He is no fool who gives what he cannot keep to gain what he cannot lose." Jesus Himself provided the ultimate example of personal sacrifice when He gave His own life for the sins of humanity. The Apostle Peter makes application to believers in his letter when he writes, "For you have been called for this purpose, since Christ also suffered for you, leaving you an example for you to follow in His steps" (1 Pet.2:21).

About Salvation

When Zaccheus repented of defrauding his fellow citizens through his abuse of Roman tax collection, Jesus announced, "Today salvation has come to this house, because he, too, is a son of Abraham. For the Son of Man has come to seek and save that which was lost" (Lk. 19:10). Jesus is the Savior who has come to provide salvation to a lost and dying humanity. Even before His birth, Joseph was told that Mary's son would be called Jesus, "for He will save His people from their sins" (Matt. 1:21). When Mary brought her son to the Jerusalem temple forty days after His birth (cf. Lev. 12:1-4), righteous Simeon took the child in his arms and thanked God saying, "My eyes have seen Your salvation, which You have prepared for all people" (Lk. 2:30). Commenting on Jesus ministry in their community, the Samaritans told the woman Jesus had encountered at Jacob's well, "It is no longer because of what you said that we believe, for we have heard for ourselves and know that this One is indeed the Savior of the world" (Jn. 4:42). Defending his preaching to the people of Jerusalem, the Apostle Peter declared to the members of the Jewish Sanhedrin, "There is salvation in no one else; for there is no other name under heaven that has been given among men by which we must be saved" (Acts 4:12).

If Jesus is the world's Savior, what do people need to be saved from? The Apostle Paul answered that question quite simply in Romans 6:23 where he wrote, "The wages of sin is death." Sin results in separation from God. If we are not saved from the outcome of our sin, our separation from God becomes eternal separation in the lake of fire where all of Satan's allies and associates will spend eternity (Rev. 20:10-15).

Jesus is the one and only Savior from an eternity without God and suffering the just consequences of our sin. This is a horrible, yet avoidable destiny. Jesus graciously offers the gift of salvation from sin and judgment for *all* who will believe. Have you received His amazing free gift?

About Satan

Jesus believed in Satan. He encountered Satan personally at the beginning of His earthly ministry when He was tempted in the wilderness (Matt. 4:1-11). Satan tempted Jesus to compromise so as to disqualify Him from fulfilling His messianic ministry. The word, "Satan," is actually a Hebrew word which means "adversary." The Greek New Testament designation for this enemy of God and His people is "devil" (*diabolos*), which means "accuser."

Satan is "the ruler of demons" (Matt. 12:24) and reigns over a counterfeit kingdom that opposes the true kingdom of God (Matt. 12:26). The parable of the sower (Matt. 13:3-9,18-23) depicts Satan as "the evil one" who "snatches away" the seed of the gospel which is sown in a person's heart. The word "Satan" can be used metaphorically when someone aligns themselves with Satan's purposes. This occurred when Peter rebuked Jesus who had announced His coming death. Jesus responded to Peter saying, "Get behind Me, Satan! You are a stumbling block to Me; for you are not setting your mind on God's interests, but man's" (Matt. 16:23).

Satan's kingdom received a significant setback when Jesus paid the penalty for humanity's sins and overcame death by His resurrection from the grave (1 Cor. 15:55, Col. 2:15). But Satan is still alive and well on planet earth, and continues to oppose God's kingdom purposes. According to Jesus, the eternal fire of hell was prepared "for the devil and his angels" (Matt. 25:41). And that is where the evil one will spend eternity (Rev. 20:10).

About the Second Coming

Jesus is coming again! The truth of His Second Coming is one of the essential doctrines of the Christian faith. On the night before His death, Jesus told His twelve apostles gathered in the upper room, "If I go and prepare a place for you, I will come again and receive you to Myself, that where I am, there you may be also" (Jn. 14:3). In His Olivet Discourse, Jesus described the events that would lead up to His Second Coming (Matt. 24:3-27). He explained that the event would take place as quick as lightning, would be clearly visible to all and accompanied by judgment (Matt. 24:27-28). After His ascension to heaven, the angels reminded Jesus' disciples of His promised return. They said, "This Jesus, who has been taken up from you into heaven, will come in just the same way as you have watched Him go into heaven" (Acts 1:11)

Some people have attempted to predict the date of Jesus' Second Coming. Jerry Falwell predicted in 1999 that Jesus' return would "probably be within ten years."

American evangelist Harold Camping announced that the Second Coming would take place on May 21, 2011. When the day passed without Jesus' appearance, he recalculated and announced October 21, 2011, as the date of the return of Jesus and destruction of the universe. We know from Scripture that Jesus will return, but nobody knows when. Speaking of His return, Jesus Himself declared, "Of that day and hour no one knows, not even the angels of heaven, nor the Son, but the Father alone" (Matt. 25:36).

About Service

Explaining the purpose of His coming to earth, Jesus told His apostles, "For even the Son of Man did not come to be served, but to serve, and to give His life a ransom for many" (Mk. 10:45). The classic example of Jesus' ministry of serving took place in the Upper Room where Jesus washed the feet of His disciples (Jn. 13:1-12). After finishing His humble service of washing dirty feet, Jesus told His disciples, "If I then, the Lord and the Teacher, washed your feet, you also ought to wash one another's feet. For I gave you an example that you also should do as I did to you" (Jn. 13:14-15).

Not everyone needs to have their feet washed. Some people just need help mowing their lawn, cleaning their gutters, or babysitting a child while they go shopping. Jesus' example in the Upper Room teaches me that my ministry is service—a humble service to others; a foot washing kind of service. Jesus told His disciples, "Whoever wishes to become great among you shall be your servant, and whoever wishes to be first among you shall be your slave." (Matt. 20:25-26). In contrast to the world's way of thinking, the great people are not those who rule, but those who serve. Not many of us will rule. But all of us can serve. And true greatness in the upside down kingdom of God comes through serving others.

About Sin

Before Jesus was born, the angel Gabriel announced to His mother, the virgin Mary, that her son would "save His people from their sins" (Matt. 1:21). If it had not been for our sins, we would not need a Savior. But what is this thing called "sin"? The Greek word for sin (*hamartia*) simply means "missing the mark." When I go target shooting, I aim for the circle, the "bull's eye," in the center of the target. If the bullet goes outside that center circle, I have "missed the mark." God's holiness is the "bull's eye" for our spiritual lives and actions. Yet, all humanity has missed the mark. The Bible calls those who have missed the mark "sinners." This is not a dismissive slam on humanity. It is just a fact that "all have sinned and fall short of the glory of God" (Rom. 3:23). And "missing the mark" has eternal consequences, for "the wages of sin is death" (Rom. 6:23).

Jesus taught that sin is a master to whom people can become enslaved (Jn. 8:34). Sin blinds us from the spiritual realities that can set us free to experience the fullness of God's blessing. Rejecting Jesus, the light of the world (Jn. 8:12), leaves people in a state of spiritual blindness (Jn. 9:39-41), separated from God and the full and abundant life He offers humanity.

The good news is that Jesus came to earth to save sinners from the eternal consequences of having "missed the mark." When Jesus was criticized by Israel's religious leaders for eating with sinners, Jesus responded saying, "It is not those who are well who need a physician, but those who are sick. I have not come to call the righteous, but sinners to repentance" (Lk. 5:31-32).

Jesus claimed divine authority to forgive sin. He told the paralyzed man, "Your sins are forgiven" (Lk. 5:20). Then He healed the man, proving His rightful authority to forgive sins. Jesus told Simon the Pharisee that the sinful woman who had washed His feet was forgiven (Lk. 7:43-48).

Luke sums up the purpose of Jesus' mission to humanity stating, that He "came to seek and to save that which was lost" (Lk. 19:10). On the night before His sacrifice on the cross, Jesus gave His disciples a symbol and a reminder of the purpose of His death. Holding up the Passover cup, Jesus said, "This is My blood of the covenant, which is poured out for many for forgiveness of sins" (Matt. 26:28). Jesus' sacrificial death is God's provision for all who have "missed the mark."

About Sinners

Jesus came to earth as Israel's promised Messiah and God's divine Son. Since God is infinitely holy (Isa. 6:3; Rev. 6:8) and hates sin (Prov. 6:16-19), we might wonder what Jesus thought about sinners. What did Jesus think about those who fall short of God's high and holy standard of righteousness?

This question was in the minds of the Pharisees and teachers of the law when they noticed how Jesus welcomed the tax collectors and others of low moral reputation at His table. Jesus responded by telling three parables (Lk. 15:3-31). He told of a shepherd who had lost one of his flock, a woman who had lost a coin and a son who had left home and squandered his inheritance. In each parable, that which was lost was sought and eventually found. In each story there is great celebration when that which was lost was found. The shepherd called his friends and said, "Rejoice with me; I have found my lost sheep" (Lk. 15:5). The woman called her friends and said, "Rejoice with me; I have found my lost coin" (Lk. 15:9). And the father provided a feast to celebrate the return of his prodigal son (Lk. 15:23-24).

These three parables reveal Jesus' attitude toward sinners. The Pharisees were no doubt surprised to learn that sinners were the special object of Jesus' affection. Rather than hating them, along with the evil they perpetuate, Jesus loves sinners and actively seeks them. In each parable, we discover the evidence of God's grace toward sinners. As the Savior of lost sinners, Jesus loved them so much that He was willing to lay down His life for them (Jn. 10:11).

About Tradition

Tevye, in the classic film, *Fiddler on the Roof*, stood precariously on a rooftop and sang, "Tradition." In the song he answers all the questions about Jewish family life with the single word, "tradition!" Tradition is not a bad thing. The Greek word (*paradosis*) refers to teaching that is passed on or delivered to others. Paul used the word to refer to the teachings he passed on to the Corinthians (1 Cor. 11:2).

Before his Damascus road encounter with Jesus, Paul was zealous for his "ancestral traditions" (Gal. 1:14). In this context, he is referring to the teachings of the rabbis which had accumulated alongside Scripture. The problem in the time of Jesus was that these Jewish traditions had become more authoritative than Scripture. The scribes and Pharisees accused Jesus' disciples of breaking "the traditions of the elders" when they didn't wash their hands in the prescribed, ceremonial manner (Matt. 15:2). There was nothing about this sort of hand washing ritual in Scripture, but it became a Jewish tradition that to eat food with unwashed hands was personally defiling.

Jesus challenged this sort of thinking by pointing out that the religious leaders have violated the command to honor their father and mother (Exod. 20:12) by the tradition of *corban*. This tradition allowed them to devote their financial resources to God to avoid helping their parents in a time of need. By doing this, Jesus said, "you invalidated the word of God for the sake of your tradition" (Matt. 15:6). The Apostle Paul warned the Colossians of the dangers of manmade traditions which are inconsistent with the teachings of Jesus (Col. 2:8). Our traditions must always be evaluated and corrected by Scripture.

About the Trinity

Jesus didn't say anything about the Trinity, and the word doesn't even appear in the Bible. But it is quite evident that Jesus believed in this doctrine. The word "Trinity," comes from "tri" (three) and "unity" (one). The doctrine of the Trinity teaches that God is *three-in-one.* God is Father, Son and Holy Spirit, three distinct persons in one God-head. This is a difficult doctrine to understand and there have been many attempts to illustrate it. Like the egg, with its three distinct parts—shell, white and yoke—so there is one, singular God with three co-equal persons. Yet this illustration is inadequate since the parts of the egg do not possess the properties or attributes of each other. Most Christians will agree that the doctrine of the Trinity, in addition to being a great mystery, is complicated!

Jesus affirmed the concept of God's *tri-unity* when He instructed His apostles to baptize new disciples "in the name of the Father and the Son and the Holy Spirit" (Matt. 28:19). The Apostle Paul embraced this doctrine as well (2 Cor. 13:14). Jesus' oneness with God is evident by His words to the Jewish leaders in Jerusalem when He said, "I and the Father are one" (Jn. 10:30). He responded to Philip's request, "Lord, show us the Father," by declaring, "He who has seen Me has seen the Father" (Jn. 14:8-9). This is consistent with the name, "Immanuel," given to Jesus in biblical prophecy (Isa. 7:14; Matt. 1:23). It means "God with us."

The doctrine of the Trinity, or God's *tri-unity*, has often led Jews and Moslems to believe that Christians worship three gods. But that would be polytheism, not biblical Christianity. In spite of the difficulty in understanding this doctrine, Jesus believed and taught that God is three-in-one. Within the one true God, there are three distinct, divine and individual persons—Father, Son and Holy Spirit.

About Works

There has been a great deal of debate over the centuries as to the place of works in God's plan of salvation. Some would argue that people earn their salvation through their good works. Others insist that works have nothing to do with salvation and that it is contrary to the doctrine of free grace to expect or suggest that Christians demonstrate their faith by their works.

While Scripture is clear that God's grace, rather than our good works, is the fundamental grounds of our salvation, Jesus recognized that one's works are an indicator of where a person is spiritually. He warned His disciples about false prophets who can be known and identified "by their fruits," that is their works (Matt. 7:16). It is not the people who say "Lord, Lord" who will enter into God's kingdom, "but he who does the will" of the Father in heaven (Matt. 7:21). But not even good works are the ultimate indicator of a person's spiritual status. Jesus told His disciples that some who had prophesied in His name, cast out demons and performed miracles would be told on the day of judgment, "I never knew you; depart from Me, you who practice lawlessness." (Matt. 7:23).

Jesus' half-brother, James, who appears to have authored the first epistle, taught that the kind of faith which has no works is not really a *saving* faith (Jms. 2:14). While good works don't save, the absence of works in a person's life is an indicator that their profession may be a fallacy. Someone has said, "Faith alone saves, but the *kind* of faith that saves is not alone." The Apostle Paul made it clear that we are saved by grace through faith, not as a result of works (Eph. 2:8-9). But then he added, "For we are His workmanship, created in Christ Jesus for good works, which God prepared beforehand so that we would walk in them" (Eph. 2:10). I don't think this truth can be expressed better than Paul did when he encouraged Titus to speak in such a way "so that those who have believed in God may devote themselves to good works" (Tit. 3:8).

About Worship

What is worship? The word simply means to "give worth" to something or someone. Worship includes adoration, praise, thanksgiving, devotion, veneration, honor, reverence, giving, praying, studying and listening to sermons. There are many different activities and contexts which are included in the concept of Christian worship. The first recorded act of worship in the New Testament was when the Magi came to Bethlehem after the birth of Jesus. Matthew records, "After coming into the house they saw the Child with Mary His mother; and they fell to the ground and worshiped Him. Then, opening their treasures, they presented to Him gifts of gold, frankincense, and myrrh" (Matt. 2:11).

During His temptation by Satan, Jesus was promised "all the kingdoms of the world" if He would only fall down and worship Satan (Matt. 4:8-9). Jesus responded by quoting the Hebrew Bible, "You shall worship the Lord your God, and serve Him only" (cf. Exod. 23:25; Deut. 6:13; 10:12). The first commandment in the "Big Ten" makes it clear that only the one, true God of Israel is worthy of our worship (Exod. 20:3). Jesus believed and obeyed that commandment.

Jesus rebuked the hypocrisy of the Jewish religious leaders whose worship was superficial. Quoting from the prophet Isaiah, Jesus said, "This people honors Me with their lips, but their heart is far away from Me. But in vain do they worship Me" (Isa. 29:13; Matt. 15:8-9). It seems that the religious leaders had mastered the *art* of worship, but didn't have the *heart* for worship. They were going through the *motions* without actually engaging their hearts in an active spirit of worship.

One of the most helpful teachings on worship appears in Jesus' conversation with the Samaritan woman whom Jesus met at Jacob's well. When the conversation with Jesus became a bit too personal, the woman attempted to change the subject. Standing there at the foot of Mt. Gerizim by Jacob's well, she said, "Our fathers worshiped in this mountain, and you people say that in Jerusalem is the place where men ought to worship" (Jn. 4:20). Both the Jews and the Samaritans were focused on the *place* of worship instead of the person of worship. Jesus announced that a time was quickly approaching when the focus on the *place* of worship--Mt. Gerizim for the Samaritans and Mt. Moriah for the Jews--would be a thing of the past.

True worship, according to Jesus, must focus on spiritual realities, not physical localities. Since God is Spirit, declared Jesus, "those who worship Him must worship in spirit and truth" (Jn. 4:24). True worship is a spiritual experience, embracing spiritual realities, and based on spiritual (biblical) truths. It is exciting to realize that God the Father actively seeks people to be His true worshipers (Jn. 4:23).

When I attend a worship service with fellow believers, I can be there strictly as an observer or as a participant. I can use the time to think about the activities of the coming week, or I can engage my mind and heart in a spirit of worship. May we, as followers of Jesus, acknowledge His worthiness as we worship our Lord and Savior in spirit and in truth.

Appendix

Time for Review:

What Does Jesus Do?

Repetition with variety is the key to learning. That is why the Hebrew word for "teaching" (*shanan*) actually means "to say again and again" or "to repeat." So in the interest of true learning, I am providing a list of the works of Jesus, starting with creation and going through eternity. This list is not complete. I am sure you can add to this list as you continue to read and study God's Word.

Jesus at Work in Eternity Past

1. Jesus created the heavens and earth. Genesis 1
2. Jesus visited with Abraham. Genesis 18
3. Jesus wrestled with Jacob. Genesis 32
4. Jesus revealed Himself to Moses. Exodus 34
5. Jesus commanded Joshua. Joshua 5
6. Jesus encouraged Gideon. Judges 6-7
7. Jesus announced the birth of Samson. Judges 13
8. Jesus called Isaiah into his ministry. Isaiah 6
9. Jesus comforted Daniel's three friends. Daniel 3
10. Jesus cleansed Israel's High Priest. Zechariah 3

Jesus at Work During His Life on Earth

1. Jesus was born of a virgin. Matthew 1
2. Jesus was approved at His baptism. Matthew 3
3. Jesus was proven through His temptation. Matthew 4
4. Jesus offered God's promised kingdom. Matthew 4
5. Jesus authenticated Himself through miracles. Matthew 4
6. Jesus preached the Sermon on the Mount. Matthew 5-7
7. Jesus was rejected by the leaders of Israel. Matthew 12
8. Jesus taught about the kingdom through parables. Matthew 13
9. Jesus was transfigured before His disciples. Matthew 17
10. Jesus entered Jerusalem as Israel's Messiah King. Matthew 21
11. Jesus made predictions about Israel's future. Matthew 24-25
12. Jesus died as a substitute for sinners. Matthew 27
13. Jesus was buried in a borrowed tomb. Matthew 27
14. Jesus was resurrected and appeared to His disciples. Matthew 28
15. Jesus returned to heaven with His earthly mission accomplished. Acts 1

Jesus at Work on Behalf of Believers Today

1. Jesus returned to heaven, renewing fellowship and work with His Father. Acts 1

2. Jesus is preparing a place in heaven for His followers. John 14
3. Jesus is officiating as high priest in heaven. Hebrews 8
4. Jesus is interceding in behalf of believers. Hebrews 7
5. Jesus is answering the prayers of His people. John 14
6. Jesus is defending believers against their accuser. 1 John 2
7. Jesus is gifting and ruling the church. Ephesians 4-5
8. Jesus is receiving worship from the heavenly court. Revelation 4

Jesus at Work in Future Prophecy

1. Jesus will meet believers at the rapture. 1Thessalonians 4
2. Jesus will initiate the tribulation judgments. Revelation 5-6
3. Jesus will return to claim His throne. Matthew 24, Revelation 19
4. Jesus will rule His promised kingdom. Revelation 20
5. Jesus will judge Satan and his followers. Revelation 20
6. Jesus will officiate judgment at the final judgment. Revelation 20
7. Jesus will comfort and bless His people. Revelation 21
8. Jesus will reverse the curse of sin. Revelation 22

9. Jesus will welcome our worship and service for eternity. Revelation 22

When I graduated from Western Seminary more than a few years ago, my father-in-law gave me an original print by the silk screen artist, Sister Corita Kent (1918-1986). She was a nun who combined pop art with messages of love, compassion and social justice. The message on my print reads, "To believe in God is to know that all the rules are fair and that there will be many wonderful surprises." I often reflect on those last words, "many wonderful surprises."

I have spent most of my lifetime studying the Bible to learn more about Jesus. While I think I know His life (past, present and future) fairly well, I am confident that there are yet to be discovered "many wonderful surprises." So, while this little book is an introduction and overview of the life of Jesus, I will conclude by encouraging you to "keep on learning." As you continue reading and studying the Bible, I believe you will discover for yourself "many wonderful surprises."

My Favorite Resources
on the Life and Ministry of Jesus

Mike Beaumont, *The One-Stop Guide to Jesus*. Lion Hudson, Oxford, England. 2010.

F. F. Bruce, *The Hard Sayings of Jesus*. InterVarsity Press. Downers Grove, IL. 1983.

Alfred Edersheim, *The Life and Times of Jesus the Messiah* (Updated Edition). Hendrickson Publishers, Peabody, MA. 1993.

David Flusser, *Jesus.* The Hebrew University Magnus Press, Jerusalem, Israel. 2001.

Michael Griffiths, *The Example of Jesus*. InterVarsity Press. Downers Grove, IL. 1985.

Harold Hoehner, *Chronological Aspects of the Life of Christ.* Zondervan Publishing House. Grand Rapids, MI. 1977

Walter C. Kaiser, Jr., *Messiah in the Old Testament.* Zondervan Publishing House. Grand Rapids, MI. 1995.

J. Carl Laney, *Discipleship: Training from the Master Disciple Maker.* Independently published. 2019.

J. Dwight Pentecost, *The Words and Works of Jesus Christ*. Zondervan, Grand Rapids, MI. 1981.

Michael Rydelnik and Edwin Blum, *The Moody Handbook of Messianic Prophecy*. Moody Publishers, Chicago, IL. 2019.

Ann Spangler and Lois Tverberg, *Sitting at the Feet of Rabbi Jesus*. Zondervan, Grand Rapids, MI. 2009.

Robert L. Thomas and Stanley N. Gundry, *The NIV Harmony of the Gospels*. HarperSanFrancisco, CA.1988.

Brad Young, *Jesus, the Jewish Theologian*. Baker Academic, Grand Rapids, MI. 1995.

Brad Young, *Meet the Rabbis: Rabbinic Thought and the Teachings of Jesus*. Hendrickson Publishers, Peabody, MA. 2007.

More Books by J. Carl Laney

The Divorce Myth (Bethany House Publishers, 1981)

First and Second Samuel (Moody Publishers, 1981)

Ezra-Nehemiah (Moody Publishers, 1982)

Zechariah (Moody Publishers, 1984)

Your Guide to Church Discipline (Bethany House, 1985)

Concise Bible Atlas (Baker, 1988)

New Bible Companion (Tyndale House, 1990)

Commentary on the Gospel of John (Moody Publishers, 1992)

Answers to Tough Questions (Kregel, 1997)

Messiah's Coming Temple (Kregel, 1997)

God (Word Publishing, 1999)

Essential Bible Background: What you should know before you read the Bible (CreateSpace, 2016)

Your Psalm of Praise (Kindle e-book, 2017)

Biblical Wisdom: Your Key to Success (CreateSpace, 2018)

Discipleship: Training from the Master Disciple Maker (CreateSpace, 2018)

The Story of Israel (Kindle Direct Publishing, 2019)

Made in the USA
Coppell, TX
27 April 2020